HEALTHY LIVING

HEALTHY LIVING

volume

3

mental health
mental illness
eating disorders
habits and behaviors
mental health therapies

Caroline M. Levchuck
Michele Drohan
Jane Kelly Kosek

Allison McNeill, Editor

AN IMPRINT OF THE GALE GROUP
DETROIT · SAN FRANCISCO · LONDON
BOSTON · WOODBRIDGE, CT

Healthy Living

Caroline M. Levchuck, Michele Drohan, Jane Kelly Kosek

STAFF

Allison McNeill, *U•X•L Senior Editor*
Carol DeKane Nagel, *U•X•L Managing Editor*
Thomas L. Romig, *U•X•L Publisher*

Margaret A. Chamberlain, *Permissions Specialist (Pictures)*

Rita Wimberley, *Senior Buyer*
Evi Seoud, *Assistant Production Manager*
Dorothy Maki, *Manufacturing Manager*
Mary Beth Trimper, *Production Director*

Michelle DiMercurio, *Senior Art Director*
Cynthia Baldwin, *Product Design Manager*

Pamela Reed, *Imaging Coordinator*
Robert Duncan, *Imaging Specialist*
Randy Bassett, *Image Database Supervisor*
Barbara Yarrow, *Graphic Services Manager*

GGS Information Services, Inc., *Typesetting*

Cover illustration by Kevin Ewing Illustrations

Library of Congress Cataloging-in-Publication Data

Levchuck, Caroline M.
  Healthy living/Caroline Levchuck, Michele Drohan.
    p. cm.
  Contents: v. 1. Nutrition, exercise, and environmental health —v.2. Medicine and healthcare —v. 3. Mental health and self-esteem.
  Includes bibliographical references and index.
  ISBN 0-7876-3918-4 (set) —ISBN 0-7876-3919-2 (v.1) —ISBN 0-7876-3920-6 (v.2) —ISBN 0-7876-3921-4 (v.3)
  1. Health–Juvenile literature. 2. Mental health–Juvenile literature. 3. Medical care–Juvenile literature. [1. Health. 2. Mental health. 3. Medical care.] I. Drohan, Michele Ingber. II. Title.
RA777.L475 2000
613–dc21   99-053258

Contents

Reader's Guide

Healthy Living covers a wide range of health-related topics and lifestyle issues in fifteen chapters spread over three volumes. Each chapter is devoted to a specific health-related topic:

- Nutrition
- Personal Care and Hygiene
- Sexuality
- Physical Fitness
- Environmental Health
- Health Care Systems
- Health Care Careers
- Preventive Care
- Over-the-Counter Drugs
- Alternative Medicine
- Mental Health
- Mental Illness
- Eating Disorders
- Habits and Behaviors
- Mental Health Therapies

Each chapter begins with a brief overview to introduce readers to the topic at hand. Paired with the overview is a chapter-specific table of contents that outlines the main sections presented within the chapter.

A "Words to Know" box included at the beginning of each chapter provides definitions of words and terms used in that chapter. At the end of each chapter, under the heading "For More Information," appears a list of books and web sites that provides students with further information about that particular topic.

Health and safety tips, historical events, and other interesting facts relating to a particular topic are presented in sidebar boxes sprinkled throughout each chapter. More than 150 photos and illustrations enhance the text.

Each volume of *Healthy Living* includes a comprehensive glossary collected from all the "Words to Know" boxes in the fifteen chapters, and ends with a general bibliography section. The offerings in the bibliography provide more general health-related sources for further information. A cumulative index providing access to all major terms and topics covered throughout *Healthy Living* concludes each volume.

Related Reference Sources

Healthy Living is only one component of the three-part U•X•L Complete Health Resource. Other titles in this library include:

- *Sick! Diseases and Disorders, Injuries and Infections.* This four-volume set contains 140 alphabetically arranged entries on diseases, disorders, and injuries, including information on their causes, symptoms, diagnoses, tests and treatments, and prognoses. Each entry, four to seven pages long, includes sidebars on related people and topics, as well as a list of sources for further research. Each volume contains a 16-page color insert. *Sick* also features more than 240 black-and-white photographs and a cumulative subject index.

- *Body by Design: From the Digestive System to the Skeleton.* This two-volume set presents the anatomy (structure) and physiology (function) of the human body in twelve chapters. Each chapter is devoted to one of the eleven organ systems that make up the body. The last chapter focuses on the special senses, which allow humans to connect with the real world. Sidebar boxes present historical discoveries, recent medical advances, short biographies of scientists, and other interesting facts. More than 100 photos, many of them in color, illustrate the text. *Body by Design* also features a cumulative index.

Acknowledgements

A note of appreciation is extended to the *Healthy Living* advisors, who provided invaluable suggestions when this work was in its formative stages:

Carole Branson
Seminar Science Teacher
Wilson Middle School
San Diego, California

Bonnie L. Raasch
Media Specialist
Vernon Middle School
Marion, Iowa

Doris J. Ranke
Science Teacher
West Bloomfield High School
West Bloomfield, Michigan

Gracious thanks to Allison McNeill, Tom Romig, and Christine Slovey as well as the rest of the U•X•L team for their patience and first-rate editorial direction. Thanks also to Leslie Levchuck, R.D., Laura Wheeldreyer, Helen Packard, Stefanie Weiss, Kristin Ward, Lynda Beauregard, Robin Mayhall, Sean G. Levchuck, M.D., and Rosemarie Rich for their expertise and contributions to this project.

Comments and Suggestions

We welcome your comments on *Healthy Living*. Please write: Editors, *Healthy Living*, U•X•L, 27500 Drake Rd., Farmington Hills, Michigan, 48331–3535; call toll free: 1–800–877–4253; fax: 248–414–5043; or send e-mail via http://www.galegroup.com.

Please Read: Important Information

Healthy Living is a medical reference product designed to inform and educate readers about health and lifestyle issues. U•X•L believes this product to be comprehensive, but not necessarily definitive. While U•X•L has made substantial efforts to provide information that is accurate and up to date, U•X•L makes no representations or warranties of any kind, including without limitation, warranties of merchantability or fitness for a particular purpose, nor does it guarantee the accuracy, comprehensiveness, or timeliness of the information contained in this product.

Readers should be aware that the universe of medical knowledge is constantly growing and changing, and that differences of medical opinion exist among authorities. They are also advised to seek professional diagnosis and treatment for any medical condition, and to discuss information obtained from this book with their health care provider.

Words to Know

A

Abscess: When pus from a tooth infection spreads to the gums.

Abstinence: Voluntary, self-denial of sexual intercourse.

Accredit: To recognize an educational institution for having the standards that allows graduates to practice in a certain field.

Acetaminophen: A generic name for a compound that affects the brain and spinal cord, altering the perception of pain and lessening it.

Acid rain: Rain with a high content of sulfuric acid.

Acupuncture: A form of alternative medicine that involves stimulating certain points, referred to as acupoints, on a person's body to relieve pain and promote healing and overall well-being.

Adaptive behavior: Things a person does to adjust to new situations.

Addiction: The state of needing to compulsively repeat a behavior.

Adrenaline: A hormone that is released during times of high pressure, stress or fear; also a chemical that blocks the histamine response in an allergic reaction.

Advocate: A person who supports or defends a cause or a proposal.

Aerobic: Something that occurs in the presence of oxygen.

Affect: An individual's emotional response and demeanor.

Affectations: Artificial attitudes or behaviors.

Allergy: A chronic condition in which an allergic reaction occurs when the immune system responds aggressively to a certain foreign substance.

Allopath: A kind of doctor who advocates the conventional system of medical practice, which makes use of all measures that have proved to be effective in the treatment of disease.

Allopathic: The system of medical practice making use of all measures that have proved to be effective in the treatment of disease.

Altered consciousness: A state of awareness that is different from typical, waking consciousness; often induced with the use of drugs and alcohol.

Alternative medicine: Medical practices that fall outside the spectrum of conventional allopathic medicine.

Alzheimer's Disease: A degenerative disease of the brain that causes people to forget things, including thought, memory, language, and the people in their lives, and which eventually leads to death. Predominantly affects the elderly.

Amenorrhea: The absence of menstrual cycles.

Anaerobic: Something that occurs without oxygen because a person is using energy to do activities at a faster rate than the body is producing it.

Analgesic: A drug that alleviates pain without affecting consciousness.

Anemia: The condition of low iron in the blood.

Anhedonia: The inability to experience pleasure.

Anorexia nervosa: A term meaning "lack of appetite"; an eating disorder marked by a person's refusal to maintain a healthy body weight through restricting food intake or other means.

Antacids: A medication used to neutralize up to 99 percent of stomach acid.

Anti-inflammatory: Chemical that counteracts inflammation.

Antibiotics: Drugs used to treat bacterial infections.

Antibodies: A substance made in the body that protects the body against germs or viruses.

Antihistamine: The drugs most commonly used to treat allergies.

Antioxidants: Powerful molecules found in certain foods and vitamins that help neutralize free radicals, which are damaging molecules.

Antipsychotic drugs: Drugs that reduce psychotic behavior, often having negative long-term side-effects.

Antiseptic: A substance that prevents the growth of germs and bacteria.

Antitussive: A type of cough medication that calms the part of the brain that controls the coughing reflex.

Anus: An opening in the body through which solid waste is expelled.

Anxiety: An abnormal and overwhelming sense of worry and fear that is often accompanied by physical reaction.

Appeal: To take a court's decision and have another higher court review it to either uphold or overturn the first decision.

Archetypes: Universally known images or symbols that predispose an individual to have a specific feeling or thought about that image.

Aromatherapy: A branch of herbal medicine that uses medicinal properties found in the essential oils of certain plants.

Art therapy: The use of art forms and craft activities to treat emotional, mental and physical disabilities.

Arthritis: Chronic inflammation of the joints; the condition causes pain and swelling.

Artificial: Human-made; not found in nature.

Asbestos: A mineral fiber.

Associate's degree: Degree granted from two-year college institutions.

Astringent: Topical solution that tightens the skin.

Attention-Deficit/Hyperactivity Disorder (ADHD): A disorder that involves difficulty in concentrating and overall inattentiveness.

Autism: A developmental disorder marked by the inability to relate socially to others and by severe withdrawal from reality. Language limitations and the extreme desire for things to remain the same are common symptoms.

Autonomy: Being in charge of oneself; independent.

B

Bachelor's degree: A four-year college degree.

Bacteria: Single-celled micro-organisms, which can be either beneficial or harmful.

Bedside manner: A physician's ability to put a patient at ease and communicate effectively.

Behavior Therapy: A form of therapy that has its history in the experimental psychology and learning processes of humans and animals. Its main focus is to change certain behaviors instead of uncovering unconscious conflicts or problems.

Behavioral Medicine: Also known as health psychology, it is another developing mental health therapy technique in the field of medicine; the interdisciplinary study of ideas and knowledge taken from medicine and behavior science.

Behaviorism: Focuses on the study of observable behavior instead of on consciousness.

Benign: Harmless; also, non-cancerous.

Binge-eating disorder: An eating disorder that involves repetitive episodes of binge eating in a restricted period of time over several months.

Bingeing: When an individual eats, in a particular period of time, an abnormally large amount of food.

Bioenergetics: Body/mind therapy that stresses the body and the mind being freed of negative actions.

Biofeedback: The technique of making unconscious or involuntary bodily processes (as heartbeats or brain waves) perceptible in order to manipulate them by conscious mental control.

Bladder: An organ that holds urine.

Blood pressure: Pressure of blood against the walls of blood vessels.

Blood vessel: Vessel through which blood flows.

Body set-point theory: Theory of weight control that claims that the body will defend a certain weight regardless of factors such as calorie intake and exercise.

Bonding: Attaching a material to the surface of a tooth for cosmetic purposes.

Brief Therapy: Also called brief psychodynamic therapy, this form of therapy involves holding therapy sessions for a briefer period of time than the classic analytical form; brief therapy focuses on the specific situations that are causing patients upset

Bulimia nervosa: A term that means literally "ox hunger"; an eating disorder characterized by a repeated cycle of bingeing and purging.

Byproduct: Something other than the main product that is produced in a chemical or biological process.

C

Caffeine: An organic compound that has a stimulating effect on the central nervous system, heart, blood vessels, and kidneys.

Calcium: A mineral in the body that makes up much of the bones and teeth, helps nerve and muscle function, as well as the body's ability to convert food into energy.

Calorie: A unit of energy contained in the food and liquids that people consume.

Capitation: An agreement between doctor and managed health care organization wherein the doctor is paid per person.

Carbohydrate: The body's primary energy source, carbohydrates are the body's fuel.

Carbon monoxide: A highly toxic, colorless, odorless gas that is produced whenever something is burned incompletely or in a closed environment.

Carcinogenic: Cancer-causing.

Carcinogens: Substance that produces cancer.

Cardiovascular fitness: How efficiently the heart and lungs can pump blood (which holds oxygen) to muscles that are being worked.

Carve out: Medical services, such as substance abuse treatment, that are separated from the rest of the services within a health care plan.

Cervix: Narrow outer end of the uterus.

Chiropractic: A way of treating certain health conditions by manipulating and adjusting the spine.

Cholera: Any of several diseases of humans and domestic animals usually marked by severe gastrointestinal symptoms.

Cholesterol: A cousin to fat, is a steroid found only in foods that come from animals, such as egg yolks, organ meats, and cheese.

Chronic condition: A condition that lasts a long time or occurs frequently (e.g., asthma). Chronic conditions can be treated but not cured.

Circumcision: The removal of the foreskin from the glans of the penis.

Classical conditioning: Learning involving an automatic response to a certain stimulus that is acquired and reinforced through association.

Clinical trial: A study that evaluates how well a new drug works, positive effects, negative side effects, and how it is best used.

Clitoris: Small erectile organ in females at front part of the vulva.

Coexisting: Existing, or occurring, at the same time.

Cognition: The grouping of the mental processes of perception, recognition, conception, judgment, and reason.

Collagen: Fibrous protein found in connective tissues such as the skin and ligaments.

Collective unconscious: According to Karl Jung, the storage area for all the experiences that all people have had over the centuries. Also present in the collective unconscious are instincts, or strong motivations that are present from birth, and archetypes.

Compulsion: Habitual behaviors or mental acts an individual is driven to perform in order to reduce stress and anxiety brought on by obsessive thoughts.

Compulsive behavior: Behavior that is repeated over and over again, uncontrollably.

Conception: Also called fertilization. The formation of a cell capable of developing into a new being, such as when a man's sperm fertilizes a woman's egg creating a human embryo.

Congenital: Existing at birth.

Conscious: According to Karl Jung, the only level of which a person is directly aware.

Contaminate: To infect something or make something unsafe for use.

Continuing education: Formal schooling above and beyond any degree that is often required of medical professionals in order to keep practicing in their specific field.

Contraception: A birth control tool that prevents conception.

Convergent thinking: Thinking that is driven by knowledge and logic (opposite of divergent thinking).

Copayment: A fixed amount of money that patients pay for each doctor's visit and for each prescription.

Correlation: The relation of two or more things that is not naturally expected.

Cortisone: A hormone from the steroid family that originates in the adrenal cortex and is known for its antiinflammatory properties.

Cosmic: Relating to the universe in contrast to Earth.

Cowper's glands: Two small glands on either side of the male urethra, below the prostate gland, that produce a clear, sticky fluid that is thought to coat the urethra for passage of sperm.

Crash(ing): Coming down from being high on drugs or alcohol.

Creativity: One's capacity to think and solve problems in a unique way.

Credentials: Proof that a person is qualified to do a job.

Cruciform: The term for certain vegetables with long stems and branching tops, such as broccoli and cauliflower.

Cunnilingus: Oral stimulation of the female genitalia (vulva or clitoris).

Cut: The practice of mixing illegal drugs with another substance to produce a greater quantity of that substance.

Cuticle: The skin surrounding the nail.

Dance therapy: The use of dance and movement to treat or alleviate symptoms associated with mental or physical illness.

Date rape: Also called acquaintance rape; forced sexual intercourse between a person and someone she or he is acquainted with, is friends with, or is dating.

Decongestant: A compound that relieves a stuffy nose by limiting the production of mucus and reducing the swelling in the mucous membrane by constricting the blood vessels in the nose, opening the airways and promoting drainage.

Deductible: The amount of money a patient must pay for services covered by the insurance company before the plan will pay for any medical bills.

Defense mechanism: The ego's unconscious way of warding off a confrontation with anxiety.

Delirium: Mental disturbance marked by confusion, disordered speech, and even hallucinations.

Delusions: False, often illogical, beliefs that an individual holds in spite of proof that his or her beliefs are untrue.

Dependent: A reliance on something or someone.

Depression: Common psychological disorder characterized by intense and prolonged feelings of sadness, hopelessness, and irritability, as well as a lack of pleasure in activities.

Detoxification: The process of freeing an individual of an intoxicating or addictive substance in the body or to free from dependence.

Diagnostic: Used to recognize a disease or an illness.

Diarrhea: An increase in the frequency, volume, or wateriness of bowel movements.

Dissertation: An in-depth research paper.

Diuretic: A drug that expels water from the body through urination.

Divergent thinking: Thinking driven by creativity (opposite of convergent thinking).

Down syndrome: A form of mental retardation due to an extra chromosome present at birth, often accompanied by physical characteristics, such as sloped eyes.

Dream analysis: A technique of Freudian therapy that involves looking closely at a patient's dreams for symbolism and significance of themes and/or repressed thoughts.

Dysfunction: The inability to function properly.

Dyslexia: A reading disorder that centers on difficulties with word recognition.

E

Echinacea: A plant (also known as purple coneflower) that herbalists believe bolsters the immune system and treats certain ailments.

Edema: Swelling.

Ego: The part of one's personality that balances the drives of the id and the exterior world that is the center of the superego.

Eidetic memory: Also known as photographic memory; the ability to take a mental picture of information and use that picture later to retrieve the information.

Ejaculation: Sudden discharge of fluid (from penis).

Electrologist: A professional trained to perform electrolysis, or the removal of hair using electric currents.

Electromagnetic: Magnetism developed by a current of electricity.

Emergency: The unexpected onset of a serious medical condition or life-threatening injury that requires immediate attention.

Emission: Substances released into the air.

Empathy: Understanding of another's situation and feelings.

Emphysema: A chronic lung disease usually caused by smoking that produces shortness of breath and relentless coughing.

Enamel: The hard outer surface of the tooth.

Endocrine disrupter: Manmade chemical that looks and acts like a naturally-occurring hormone but which disturb the functioning of the naturally-occurring hormone.

Endometrial: Referring to mucous membrane lining the uterus.

Endorphin: Any of a group of natural proteins in the brain known as natural painkillers that make people feel good after exercising and act as the body's natural pain reliever.

Endurance: A person's ability to continue doing a stressful activity for an extended period of time.

Enema: A process that expels waste from the body by injecting liquid into the anus.

Enuresis: The inability to control one's bladder while sleeping at night; commonly known as bed-wetting.

Environmental tobacco smoke (ETS): The mixture of the smoke from a lit cigarette, pipe, or cigar and the smoke exhaled by the person smoking; commonly known as secondhand smoke or passive smoking.

Enzyme: A complex protein found in the cells that acts as a catalyst for chemical reactions in the body.

Ephedra: A type of plant (also known as Ma Huang) used to treat ailments, including bronchial problems, and as a decongestant.

Epidemic: The rapid spreading of a disease to many people at the same time.

Epidemiology: The study of disease in a population.

Epididymis: System of ducts leading from the testes that holds sperm.

Esophagus: The muscular tube that connects the throat with the stomach.

Estrogen: Hormone that stimulates female secondary sex characteristics.

Euphoric: Having the feeling of well-being or elation (extreme happiness).

Exercise: A subset of physical activity, which is an activity that is structured and planned.

Exercise addiction: Also known as compulsive exercise, a condition in which participation in exercise activities is taken to an extreme; an individual exercises to the detriment of all other things in his or her life.

Existential therapy: Therapy that stresses the importance of existence and urges patients to take responsibility for their psychological existence and well-being.

Expectorant: A type of cough medication that helps clear the lungs and chest of phlegm.

Extrovert: Being outgoing and social.

F

Fallopian tubes: Pair of tubes that conducts the egg from the ovary to the uterus .

Fat: Part of every cell membrane and the most concentrated source of energy in one's diet, fat is used by the body to insulate, cushion, and support vital organs.

Fee-for-service: When a doctor or hospital is paid for each service performed.

Fellatio: Oral stimulation of the male genitalia.

Fellowship: Advanced study and research that usually follows a medical residency.

Feverfew: An herb used to treat migraines.

Fluoride: A chemical compound that is added to toothpaste and drinking water to help prevent tooth decay.

Formulary: A list of prescription drugs preferred by a health plan for its members.

Free radicals: Harmful molecules in the body that damage normal cells and can cause cancer and other disorders.

Fungus: An organism of plant origin that lacks chlorophyll; some fungi cause irritation or disease (a mold is a kind of fungus).

G

Gallstone: Stones made up of cholesterol or calcium that form in the gall-bladder.

Generic drug: A drug that is approved by the Food and Drug Administration but does not go by a specific brand name and therefore is less expensive than a brand name drug.

Genetic: Something present in the genes that is inherited from a person's biological parents; hereditary.

Genetic predisposition: To be susceptible to something because of genes.

Genitalia: The reproductive organs.

Geriatric: Elderly.

Gestalt therapy: A humanistic therapy that urges individuals to satisfy growing needs, acknowledge previously unexpressed feelings, and reclaim facets of their personalities that have been denied.

Gingivitis: An inflammation of the gums that is the first stage of gum disease.

Ginkgo biloba: A tree (the oldest living kind of tree, in fact) whose leaves are believed to have medicinal value, particularly in aiding memory and treating dizziness, headaches, and even anxiety.

Ginseng: An herb used as a kind of cureall, with benefits to the immune system and aiding the body in coping with stress. Some also believe it aids concentration.

Gland: A part of the body that makes a fluid that is either used or excreted by the body; glands make sweat and bile.

H

Habit: A behavior or routine that is repeated.

Halitosis: Chronic bad breath caused by poor oral hygiene, illness, or another condition.

Hallucination: The illusion of seeing or hearing something that does not really exist; can occur because of nervous system disorders or in response to drugs.

Hangnail: Loose skin near the base of the nail.

Hangover: The syndrome that occurs after being high on drugs or drinking alcohol, often including nausea, headache, dizziness, and fuzzy-mindedness.

Health Maintenance Organization (HMO): A health plan that generally covers preventive care, such as yearly checkups and immunizations. Care must be provided by a primary care physician and services must be approved by the plan in order to be covered.

Heart disease: When arteries become clogged with a fatty buildup; this can cause a heart attack or a stroke.

Heat stroke: A serious condition that causes the body to stop sweating and overheat dangerously.

Hemoglobin: A protein found in red blood cells, needed to carry oxygen to the body's many tissues.

Hemorrhoids: A form of varicose veins that occurs when the veins around the anus become swollen or irritated.

Hepatitis: One of several severe liver-damaging diseases specified by the letters A, B, C and D.

Herbicide: A chemical agent used to kill damaging plants, such as weeds.

Histamines: Chemicals released in an allergic reaction that cause swelling of body tissues.

Holistic: Of or relating to the whole rather than its parts; holistic medicine tries to treat both the mind and the body.

Homeopathy: A kind of alternative medicine that employs natural remedies.

Hormone: Substances found in the body's glands that control some of the body's functions, such as growth.

Humane: Marked by compassion or sympathy for other people or creatures.

Humanistic: A philosophy that places importance on human interests and dignity, stressing the individual over the religious or spiritual.

Hymen: Fold of mucous membrane partly closing the orifice of the vagina.

Hypertension: High blood pressure.

Hypnosis: A trance-like state of consciousness brought about by suggestions of relaxation, which is marked by increased suggestibility.

Hypoallergenic: Unlikely to cause an allergic reaction.

Hypothesize: To make a tentative assumption or educated guess in order to draw out and test its logical or observable consequences.

I

Ibuprofen: The generic name for a type of analgesic that works in the same manner as aspirin but can be used in instances when aspirin cannot.

Id: According to Sigmund Freud, the biological instincts that revolve around pleasure, especially sexual and aggressive impulses.

Identical twins: Also called monozygotic twins; twins born from the same egg and sperm.

Immune system: The body's own natural defenses against germs and other infectious agents; protects the body against illness.

Immunization: The introduction of disease-causing compounds into the body in very small amounts in order to allow the body to form antigens against the disease.

Incinerator: A machine that burns waste materials.

Indemnity plan: A plan in which the insurance company sets a standard amount that it will pay for specific medical services.

Indigenous: Occurring naturally in an environment.

Industrial: Relating to a company that manufactures a product.

Inert: A chemical agent lacking in active properties.

Infection: A disease that is caused by bacteria.

Infinitesimals: Immeasurably small quantity or variable.

Inhalants: Substances that people sniff to get high.

Inherent: Belonging to the essential nature of something.

Innate: Inborn; something (a characteristic) a person is born with.

Insight therapy: A group of different therapy techniques that assume that a person's behavior, thoughts, and emotions become disordered as a result of the individual's lack of understanding as to what motivates him or her.

Insomnia: Chronic sleeplessness or sleep disturbances.

Insulin: The substance in the body that regulates blood sugar levels.

Intelligence: The ability and capacity to understand.

Intelligence Quotient (IQ): A standardized measure of a person's mental ability as compared to those in his or her age group.

Interaction: When two drugs influence the effects of each other.

Internalized: To incorporate something into one's self.

Internship: Supervised practical experience.

Intestinal: Having to do with the intestine, the part of the body that digests food.

Introvert: Being quiet and soft-spoken.

Iridology: The study of the iris of the eye in order to diagnose illness or disease.

Iron-deficiency anemia: When the body is lacking in the right amount of red blood cells, caused by a deficiency of iron.

Irrational: Lacking reason or understanding.

K

Keratin: A tough protein produced by the body that forms the hair and nails.

Kidney stone: Stones made of calcium or other minerals that form in the kidney or the ureter, which leads to the bladder.

Kinesiology: The study of anatomy in relation to movement of the body.

Kleptomania: Habitual stealing or shoplifting.

L

Labia majora: Outer fatty folds of the vulva (big lips).

Labia minora: Inner connective folds of the vulva (little lips).

Lanugo: Fine hair that grows all over the body to keep it warm when the body lacks enough fat to accomplish this.

Larynx: The voice box.

Laxatives: Drugs that induces bowel movements and alleviate constipation, or the inability to have a bowel movement.

Leaching: The process of dissolving outward by the action of a permeable substance.

Lead: A heavy, flexible, metallic element that is often used in pipes and batteries.

Learning: Modifying behavior and acquiring new information or skills.

Learning disorders: Developmental problems relating to speech, academic, or language skills that are not linked to a physical disorder or mental retardation.

Licensed: Authorization to practice a certain occupation.

M

Mantra: A phrase repeated during meditation to center the mind.

Manual: Involving the hands.

Massage therapy: The manipulation of soft tissue in the body with the aim of relieving and preventing pain, stress, and muscle spasms.

Master's degree: A college degree that ranks above a four-year bachelor's degree.

Masturbation: Erotic stimulation of one's own genitals.

Maturation: Process of becoming mature; developing, growing up.

Medicaid: The joint state-federal health care program for low-income people.

Medicare: The federal health insurance program for senior citizens.

Medigap: Private insurance that helps pay for some of the costs involved in Medicare.

Meditation: The act of focusing on one's own thoughts for the purpose of relaxation.

Memory: The ability to acquire, store, and retrieve information.

Menstruation: Monthly discharge of blood and tissue debris from the uterus.

Metabolism: The rate at which the body uses energy.

Microscopic: Invisible without the use of a microscope, an instrument that enlarges images of tiny objects.

Mineral: A nutrient that helps regulate cell function and provides structure for cells.

Modeling: Learning based on modeling one's behavior on that of another person with whom an individual strongly identifies.

Monosodium glutamate (MSG): A substance that enhances flavor but causes food intolerance in some people.

Mortality: The number of deaths in a given time or place.

Mucous membranes: The lining of the nose and sinus passages that helps shield the body from allergens and germs.

Mucus: A slippery secretion that is produced by mucous membranes, which it moistens and protects.

Musculoskeletal: Relating to the muscles and bones.

Music therapy: The use of music to treat or alleviate symptoms associated with certain mental or physical illnesses.

N

National health care system: A system in which the government provides medical care to all its citizens.

Nature: The biological or genetic makeup of a person.

Naturopathy: A kind of alternative medicine that focuses on the body's inherent healing powers and works with those powers to restore and maintain overall health.

Neurons: Nerve cells that receive chemical-electrical impulses from the brain.

Neurosis: An emotional disorder that produces fear and anxiety.

Neurotransmitters: A substance that transmits nerve impulses.

Nicotine: An organic compound in tobacco leaves that has addictive properties.

Nitrogen dioxide: A gas that cannot be seen or smelled. It irritates the eyes, ears, nose, and throat.

Noninvasive: Not involving penetration of the skin.

Nonproductive cough: A dry and hacking cough.

Nurture: How a person is raised, by whom, and in what environment.

Nutrient: Food substances that nourish the body.

O

Obesity: The condition of being very overweight.

Observational learning: Learning by observing the behavior of others.

Obsessions: Repeating thoughts, impulses, or mental images that are irrational and which an individual cannot control.

Off-label drug: A drug that is not formally approved by the Food and Drug Administration but is approved for legal use in some medical treatments.

Operant conditioning: Learning involving voluntary response to a certain stimuli based on positive or negative consequences resulting from the response.

Oral sex: Sexual activity involving the mouth.

Organic: Occurring naturally.

Orgasm: The peak or climax of sexual excitment.

Osteopathy: A system of medical practice based on the theory that disease is due chiefly to mechanical misalignment of bones or body parts.

Osteoporosis: A degenerative bone disease involving a decrease in bone mass, making bones more fragile.

Ova: Female reproductive cells; also called eggs.

Ovaries: Female reproductive organs that produce eggs and female sex hormones.

Overdose: A dangerous, often deadly, reaction to taking too much of a certain drug.

Ovulation: Discharge of mature ovum from the ovary.

Ozone layer: The atmospheric shield that protects the planet from harmful ultraviolet radiation.

P

Palpitation: Rapid, irregular heartbeat.

Panacea: A cure-all.

Parasites: Any plant or animal that lives on or in another plant or animal and gets food from it at the expense of its host.

Parkinson's disease: A progressive disease that causes slowing and stiffening of muscular activity, trembling hands, and a difficulty in speaking and walking.

Particle: A microscopic pollutant released when fuel does not burn completely.

Penis: Male sex organ and channel by which urine and ejaculate leave the body.

Perception: One's consciousness and way of observing things.

Periodontal disease: Gum disease, the first stage of which is gingivitis.

Person-Centered Therapy: A form of therapy put forth by Carl Rogers that looks at assumptions made about human nature and how we can try to understand them. It posits that people should be responsible for themselves, even when they are troubled.

Personal unconscious: According to Karl Jung, the landing area of the brain for the thoughts, feelings, experiences, and perceptions that are not picked up by the ego.

Personality: All the traits and characteristics that make people unique.

Pesticide: A chemical agent used to kill insects and other pests.

Pharmacotherapy: The use of medication to treat emotional and mental problems.

Phenylpropanolamine (PPA): A chemical that disrupts the hunger signals being sent by the brain; it is often used in weight loss aids.

Phlegm: Sticky mucus present in the nose, throat, and lungs.

Phobia: A form of an anxiety disorder that involves intense and illogical fear of an object or situation.

Physical activity: Any movement that spends energy.

Physiological: Relating to the functions and activities of life on a biological level.

Physiology: A branch of science that focuses on the functions of the body.

Pinna: Outer part of the ear; part of the ear that is visible.

Plaque: A sticky film of bacteria that grows around the teeth.

Plaster: A medicated or protective dressing that consists of a film (as of cloth or plastic) usually spread with a medicated substance.

Point of service (POS): A health plan in which members can see the doctor of their choosing at the time they need to see a doctor.

Pores: Small openings in the skin.

Post-Traumatic Stress Disorder (PTSD): Reliving trauma and anxiety related to an event that occurred earlier.

Potassium: A chemical element that is a silver-white, soft metal occurring in nature.

Predisposition: To be susceptible to something.

Preferred provider organization (PPO): A health plan in which members have their health care paid for only when they choose from a network of doctors and hospitals.

Premium: Fee paid for a contract of insurance.

Preventive care: Medical care that helps to maintain one's health, such as regular checkups.

Primary care physician: The doctor who is responsible for the total care of a patient and has the ability to refer patients to other doctors or specialists.

Pro-choice: Supports a woman's choice in regard to abortion.

Productive cough: A cough that brings up phlegm.

Prohibition: An era in the 1920s when alcohol was made illegal.

Prostaglandin: A hormonelike substance that affects blood vessels and the functions of blood platelets, and sensitizes nerve endings to pain.

Prostate gland: A muscular glandular body situated at the base of the male urethra.

Protein: An organic substance made of amino acids that are necessary for human life.

Protozoan: One-celled organism that can cause disease in humans.

Psychiatry: The branch of medicine that relates to the study and treatment of mental illness.

Psychoactive: Something that affects brain function, mood and behavior.

Psychoanalysis: A theory of psychotherapy, based on the work of Sigmund Freud, involving dream analysis, free association, and different facets of the self (id, ego, superego).

Psychodrama: A therapy that involves a patient enacting or reenacting life situations in order to gain insight and alter behavior. The patient is the actor while the therapist is the director.

Psychodynamics: The forces (emotional and mental) that develop in early childhood and how they affect behavior and mental well-being.

Psychological vulnerability: Used to describe individuals who are potential candidates for drug addiction because of prior experiences or other influences.

Psychology: The scientific study of mental processes and behaviors.

Psychophysical energy: Energy made up of energy from the body and the mind.

Psychotherapy: The general term of an interaction in which a trained mental health professional tries to help a patient resolve emotional and mental distress.

Puberty: The onset of sexual maturation in young adults; usually between the ages of 13 and 16 in males and 12 and 15 in females.

Purging: When a person gets rid of the food that she has eaten by vomiting, taking an excessive amount of laxatives, diuretics, or enemas or engaging in fasting and/or excessive exercise.

Pyromania: Habitual need to start fires.

Q

Qi (or Chi): Life energy vital to an individual's well-being.

R

Radiation: Energy or rays emitted when certain changes occur in the atoms or molecules of an object or substance.

Radon: A colorless, odorless, radioactive gas produced by the naturally occurring breakdown of the chemical element uranium in soil or rocks.

RapidEye Movement (REM) sleep: A deep stage of sleep during which time people dream.

Rational-emotive behavior therapy: Therapy that seeks to identify a patient's irrational beliefs as the key to changing behavior rather than examining the cause of the conflict itself.

Rationing: The process of limiting certain products or services because of a shortage.

Reality therapy: A therapy that empowers people to make choices and control their own destinies.

Referral: Permission from the primary care physician to see another doctor.

Reflexology: A type of alternative medicine that involves applying pressure to certain points, referred to as reflex points, on the foot.

Registered: To complete the standards of education issued by a state government to practice a certain profession.

Rehabilitation: To restore or improve a condition of health or useful activity.

Reimbursement plan: A plan where a patient must pay for medical services up front and then get paid back from the insurance company.

Reinforcement: Making something stronger by adding extra support.

Remorse: Ill feelings stemming from guilt over past actions.

Residency: Advanced training in a medical specialty that includes or follows a physician's internship.

Residential treatment: Treatment that takes place in a facility in which patients reside.

Right-to-life: Supports anti-abortion (with possible exceptions for incest and rape) movement.

Ritual: Observances or ceremonies that mark change, renewal, or other events.

Russell's sign: Calluses, cuts, and sores on the knuckles from repeated self-induced vomiting.

S

St. John's Wort: An herb used as an antiinflammatory drug, to treat depression, and as an analgesic.

Saturated fat: Fat that is solid at room temperature.

Savant: A person with extensive knowledge in a very specific area.

Schizophrenia: A chronic psychological disorder marked by scattered, disorganized thoughts, confusion, and delusions.

Scrotum: External pouch that contains the testes.

Sebum: An oily substance that lubricates the hair shaft.

Secondhand smoke: Also known as environmental tobacco smoke (ETS). The mixture of the smoke from a lit cigarette, pipe, or cigar and the smoke exhaled by the person smoking.

Sectarian medicine: Medical practices not based on scientific experience; also known as alternative medicine.

Self-esteem: How an individual feels about her or himself.

Self-medicate: When a person treats an ailment, mental or physical, with alcohol or drugs rather than seeing a physician or mental health professional.

Sexual abuse: All levels of sexual contact against anyone's will, including inappropriate touching, kissing, and intercourse.

Sexual harassment: All unwanted and unsolicited sexual advances, talk, and behavior.

Sexual intercourse: Involves genital contact between individuals.

Side effect: A secondary (and usually negative) reaction to a drug.

Smegma: Cheesy sebaceous matter that collects between the penis and the foreskin.

Social Security: A government program that provides economic security to senior citizens and the disabled.

Social norms: Things that are standard practices for the larger part of society.

Somatogenesis: Having origins from within the body, as opposed to the mind.

Specialist: A doctor who concentrates on only one area of medicine, such as a dermatologist (skin specialist).

Specialize: To work in a special branch of a certain profession.

Sperm: Male reproductive cell.

Sterilization: A process that makes something free of living bacteria.

Stimulant: Substance that excites the nervous system and may produce a temporary increase in ability.

Stimulus: Something that causes action or activity.

Stressor: Something (for example, an event) that causes stress.

Stroke: A sudden loss of consciousness, feeling, and voluntary movement caused by a blood clot in the brain.

Subatomic: Relating to particles smaller than atoms.

Suicide: Taking one's own life.

Sulfur dioxide: A toxic gas that can also be converted to a colorless liquid.

Superego: According to Sigmund Freud, the part of one's personality that is concerned with social values and rules.

Suppress: To stop the development or growth of something.

Symptom: Something that indicates the presence of an illness or bodily disorder.

Synapse: Gaps between nerves; the connections between neurons that allow people to make mental connections.

Synthetic: Human-made; not found in nature.

T

Temperament: How a person behaves.

Tendinitis: Inflammation of a tendon.

Testicles: Male reproductive gland that produces sperm.

Testosterone: Hormone produced by testes.

Thyroid: A gland that controls the growth of the body

Tic: A quirk of behavior or speech that happens frequently.

Tolerance: The build-up of resistance to the effects of a substance.

Topical: Designed for application on the body.

Tourette's Disorder: A disorder marked by the presence of multiple motor tics and at least one vocal tic, as well as compulsions and hyperactivity.

Toxic: Relating to or caused by a poison

Toxins: Poisonous substances.

Transference: A patient's responses to an analyst that are not in keeping with the analyst-patient relationship but seem instead to resemble ways of behaving toward significant people in the patient's past.

Transient: Passes quickly into and out of existence.

U

Ultrasound: The use of high-frequency sound waves that forms an image to detect a problem in the body.

Unsaturated fat: Fat that is liquid at room temperature, like vegetable oil.

Uranium: A chemical element that is a silver-white, hard metal and is radioactive.

Urethra: The tube from the bladder to outside the body through which urine is expelled.

Uterus: Womb; female organ that contains and nourishes an embryo/fetus.

V

Vaccine: A substance made up of weak bacteria and put into the body to help prevent disease.

Vagina: The female canal that leads from the cervix (or opening of the uterus) to the vulva (or the external female genitalia).

Vas deferens: Spermatic duct connected to the epididymis and seminal vesicle.

Vasoconstrictor: A drug that constricts the blood vessels to affect the blood pressure.

Vegan: A strict vegetarian who doesn't eat any animal by-products or any dairy.

Vegetarian: A person who lives on a diet free of meat products; some vegetarians will eat eggs or dairy products, while others will not.

Veneer: A covering, often made of porcelain, that is placed over a tooth that is damaged or for cosmetic reasons.

Vertebra: A bony piece of the spinal column fitting together with other vertebrae to allow flexible movement of the body. (The spinal cord runs through the middle of each vertebra.)

Virus: A tiny organism that causes disease.

Vitamin: A nutrient that enables the body to use fat, protein, and carbohydrates effectively.

Volatile organic compound (VOC): An airborne chemical that contains carbon.

W

Withdrawal: The phase of removal of drugs or alcohol from the system of the user.

Y

Yeast infection: A common infection of a woman's vagina caused by overgrowth of the yeast Candida Albicans.

Yoga: A form of exercise and a system of health that involves yoga postures to promote well-being of body and mind through regulated breathing, concentration, and flexibility.

HEALTHY LIVING

11

Mental Health

One of the most studied and, at times, most misunderstood phenomena of biology (study of living organisms) and psychology (study of the mind) is how people develop mentally: how do people become who they are? How do individuals develop the capacity for learning, memory, intelligence, and personality? Why do two or more individuals, born to and reared by the same parents (and therefore possessing similar genetic makeup to their siblings), often turn out to be individuals with such different likes and dislikes, different strengths and weaknesses? Why do some people develop mental illness while their brothers or sisters do not?

As with most studies pertaining to the mind, there are not many hard and fast answers. Scientists, doctors, and mental health professionals have different theories as to how people develop and grow mentally. Some theorists believe that the environment in which a person is raised contributes not only to one's personality but also to overall intelligence, and can even foster or prevent the development of certain mental illness. Still other scientists propose that biology plays a bigger role than environment and people develop as they are genetically programmed to do. For the most part, those in the field of mental health and development research take into account both biological and environmental factors as equally important in the development and growth of the mind.

This chapter will discuss the different areas of development that contribute to the whole of mental health, including identity and personality, memory, learning, intelligence, creativity, and self-esteem. Together, these areas are the things that make people who they are.

NATURE VS. NURTURE: DOES BIOLOGY OR ENVIRONMENT INFLUENCE DEVELOPMENT?

The nature vs. nurture debate revolves around the following question: what factors contribute to the mental development of an individual: nature (that is, the biological or genetic makeup of a person) or nurture (that is, how a person is raised, by whom, and in what environment)? Just as human beings inherit certain physical traits from their biological parents (such as height, eye color, and even predisposition to physical ailments), human beings can also inherit certain mental characteristics and traits from their parents, such as a propensity for certain mental disorders. What else is inherited and what traits and characteristics develop as a result of the environment in which an individual is raised? Some researchers believe that things such

WORDS TO KNOW

Alzheimer's disease: A degenerative disease of the brain that causes people to forget things, including the people in their lives, and which eventually leads to death.

Autonomy: Being in charge of oneself; independent.

Classical conditioning: Learning involving an automatic response to a certain stimulus that is acquired and reinforced through association.

Convergent thinking: Thinking that is driven by knowledge and logic (opposite of divergent thinking).

Creativity: One's capacity to think and solve problems in a unique way.

Divergent thinking: Thinking driven by creativity (opposite of convergent thinking).

Eidetic memory: Also known as photographic memory; the ability to take a mental picture of information and use that picture later to retrieve the information.

Extrovert: Being outgoing and social.

Identical twins: Also called monozygotic twins; twins born from the same egg and sperm.

Innate: Inborn; something (a characteristic) a person is born with.

Intelligence: The ability and capacity to understand.

Intelligence Quotient (IQ): The measure of intelligence as based on intelligence tests and the intelligence of the general population.

Introvert: Being quiet and soft-spoken.

Learning: Modifying behavior and acquiring new information or skills.

Memory: The ability to acquire, store, and retrieve information.

Modeling: Learning based on modeling one's behavior on that of another person with whom an individual strongly identifies.

Nature: The biological or genetic makeup of a person.

Neurons: Nerve cells that receive chemical-electrical impulses from the brain.

Nurture: How a person is raised, by whom, and in what environment.

Observational learning: Learning from the examples of others.

Operant conditioning: Learning involving voluntary response to a certain stimuli based on positive or negative consequences resulting from the response.

Personality: All the traits and characteristics that make people unique.

Reinforcement: Making something stronger by adding extra support.

Self-esteem: How an individual feels about her or himself.

Stimulus: Something that causes action or activity.

Synapse: Gaps between nerves; the connections between neurons that allow people to make mental connections.

Temperament: How people behave.

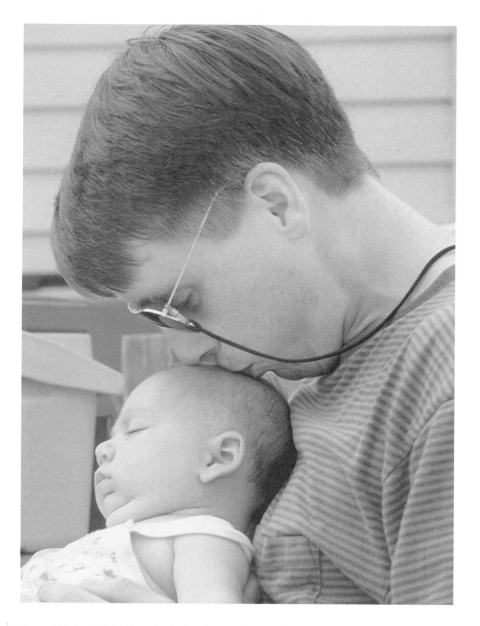

Time will tell which traits—physical and mental—this father has passed along to his son. (Photograph by Robert J. Huffman. Field Mark Publications. Reproduced by permission.)

as alcoholism or even intelligence are biologically inherited while other people support the theory that many of these things are a product of the environment in which an individual is raised.

Many studies in the nature versus nurture conflict center on identical twins. Researchers look not only at twins raised together but those raised apart to determine whether or not a certain trait is biologically programmed or if it evolves as a result of the environment in which one twin was raised. However, a flaw in research of this type is that, often times, the twins who had been separated by adoption were raised in very similar environments.

Intelligence

The most controversial area in the nature vs. nurture debate is intelligence. The reason for this may be that intelligence (which is a person's capacity to think rationally and deal with challenges effectively) is closely related to achievement, both scholastic and in other situations. While most researchers agree that intelligence is influenced by genetics to a great degree, studies show that twins of all kinds and biological siblings are more likely to possess similar intelligence. In fact, the closer the biological link, the stronger the similarity in intelligence. However, there are also similarities in intelligence between unrelated children raised together in the same household, though these similarities are not as great as those between biological siblings and, especially, twins.

What this and other similar research says is that no one definitive factor solely affects intelligence. The manner in which an individual is raised greatly influences one's intelligence. While one researcher, psychologist Arthur Jensen, put forth that intelligence is 80 percent determined by biological factors, other researchers have settled upon figures ranging between 50 and 70 percent. This means that whatever an individual's natural intelligence, it can always be improved or obstructed by his or her environment.

Personality

In addition to physical characteristics and intelligence, researchers have also tried to determine whether genetics or the environment influences an individual's personality. If a really outgoing, social individual has a child, will that child also be outgoing? Some researchers say yes. In fact, scientists have been able to prove that there is a biological relationship in terms of personality where extroversion (being outgoing and social) and neuroticism (being touchy, moody, or overly sensitive) are concerned.

How can this be proven? Through studies involving twins living apart. In fact, similar studies have found that many things seem to be inherited—from values and political attitudes to

This young man has been encouraged by his parents to read the newspaper each day, thus boosting his intelligence. (Photograph by Robert J. Huffman. Field Mark Publications. Reproduced by permission.)

the amount of time people spend watching television! This may sound silly and, of course, no one is suggesting that a specific gene has evolved that directly influences a person's preference for watching television. Rather, what researchers are focusing on is that the act of watching television is usually a solitary, passive one. This could be something that is tied to whether or not a person is extroverted. Findings of this type are also confirmed by the fact that scientists have identified a gene that affects brain chemistry and may be the reason that certain individuals engage in risk-taking behaviors, such as bungee jumping or extreme sports, while others do not.

Mental Disorders

As discussed in Chapter 12 on Mental Illness, schizophrenia (a serious psychological disorder marked by scattered thoughts, confusion, and delusions) has been found to have a high genetic correlation, meaning that if one family member has schizophrenia, there is an increased likelihood that another family member (or future offspring) may also develop it. Of course, while an individual may be predisposed to schizophrenia because of genetics, that is not to say that he will ever develop the disorder. Other psychological disorders that may be hereditary include alcoholism and major depression. [See Chapter 12: Mental Illness.]

Most researchers now agree to some extent that both biology and environment play important roles in shaping people. Just as children may share traits with biological parents, adopted children may also share many traits and habits with their adoptive parents. What this information serves to do is help mental health professionals, teachers, and researchers help all people realize their potential for growth and accomplishment in their lives.

BECOMING AN INDIVIDUAL: PERSONALITY, INDIVIDUALITY, AND TEMPERAMENT

All people have completely unique behavioral traits, likes and dislikes, and habits that make them who they are. This uniqueness comes not only from biological factors, such as temperament, but is also developed from experiences, such as a person's sense of individuality, or a combination of both environmental and biological factors, such as personality.

Personality

Personality refers to all of the traits and characteristics individuals show the world, and which make them different from others. In fact, the word personality comes from a Latin term meaning "mask." As stated in Chapter 12 on Mental Illness, people who have extreme personalities often have personality disorders. However, most people have a personality type that does not prevent them from functioning effectively within society. For example,

Even among siblings, different personalities make everyone unique. (Photograph by Robert J. Huffman. Field Mark Publications. Reproduced by permission.)

some people may be naturally more self-involved than others. These people may have a narcissistic personality type, meaning they are driven more by their own needs and desires than others are; however, this does not mean that they are dysfunctional in any way. Some people may desire close relationships with others and base much of what they do on the opinions of those other people. These individuals may have a dependent personality type; again, though, this is not necessarily an indication of dysfunction.

Some people are extroverted (outgoing) while others are introverted (shy, reserved). Some people are optimistic (positive) while others tend to be more negative, seeing the downside of situations rather than the upside. The type of personality a person has can, according to certain mental health professionals, cause him or her to seek out certain situations that agree with his view of the world and personality. This results in a certain consistency, in which the personality drives decisions that reinforce a person's personality.

Individuality

As personality begins to develop, it is reinforced and solidified during adolescence when young people begin to ask the question, "Who am I?". This quest for and achievement of individuality is perhaps best illustrated by looking at the work of renowned psychoanalytic theorist Erik Erikson (1902–1994), who mapped out an eight-stage process that covered all stages of development, with the stages in adolescence focusing on identity and individuality.

Erikson's stages include stage one, "basic trust versus mistrust," which takes place in infancy and usually centers on an infant learning trust through being cared for properly. In the toddler years, stage two, the "autonomy (independence) versus shame and doubt" stage, is resolved by allowing a child to assert independence and not feel bad for misbehaving or failing at his attempts at independence (toilet training, etc.). Stage three consists of a conflict related to "initiative versus guilt" in early childhood; at this time children begin to act on curiosities and explore new things, and the conflict is resolved if children are encouraged in their new interests and curiosities. In middle childhood stage four emerges, involving "industry versus inferiority"; and during this stage a child must achieve things (do homework, acquire skills) in order to avoid feeling inferior (less worthy than others).

Stage five, a pivotal stage in terms of this discussion, involves "identity versus role confusion" in the teen years. During this time, adolescents attempt to form their own personal identity based on who they were in childhood and where they wish to go personally and professionally in the future. What can happen at this stage, though, is that a teen who prematurely sets himself in a certain identity is at risk for having grasped onto a persona that is based on the approval of friends. Thus, this teen may be less autonomous (independent) and inquisitive (eager to learn) than others. All of this can lead to the formation of an individual who is not open to change and new experiences.

BABIES AND TEMPERAMENT

People often make statements about others such as, "He was born happy," or "She's always been moody; she's been that way since birth." This may seem like an exaggeration, but, according to many theorists, this is explained by temperament. Alexander Thomas and Stella Chess, pioneers in the field of temperament, describe temperament as how people behave. How active is a child naturally? How does the child adapt to change? How energetic is a child? How responsive? All of these things, according to researchers, are genetically programmed for the most part.

Temperament could account for the dramatic differences in siblings' behaviors from infancy. Some infants are naturally "easy babies," with positive dispositions and who adapt and adjust easily, while other infants are categorized as "difficult babies" who are moody and easily irritated.

Researchers have put forth that, generally, temperament remains constant throughout the span of an individual's life.

Another problem that can arise in Erikson's fifth stage of development is identity confusion. Erikson is referring to teens who simply are never certain of who they are. When this happens, a young person runs the risk of being unable to forge meaningful relationships and possibly alienating others with immature behavior and reasoning.

For all of these reasons, it is imperative that children and young adults be encouraged to figure out their likes and dislikes, talents and natural inclinations, and to try new things during the development process so that they will develop a sense of identity.

Stage six is concerned with the conflict of "intimacy versus isolation" stage during early adulthood. During this time, people seek out deep, meaningful intimate relationships or choose to isolate themselves, possibly with

Individuals with positive self-esteem believe that they measure up to others sufficiently. They are more likely to have the confidence to pursue different accomplishments, such as taking up a musical instrument. (Photograph by Robert J. Huffman. Field Mark Publications. Reproduced by permission.)

very negative consequences later in life. Stage seven presents itself in a conflict of "generativity versus stagnation," meaning that people should feel that they have contributed to the development of other people, particularly young people, or they will be left feeling the effects of stagnation (not changing or growing), which is the opposite of generativity (growth or creativity).

The last stage, stage eight, plays out in late adulthood in the way of "ego integrity versus despair." At this stage, adults reflect on the lives they have led, evaluating whether they have accomplished something with their lives and choices and whether they have contributed to the betterment of society.

MEMORY

Memory is one of the most important functions of the brain. Whether people realize it or not, their memories define who they are. Without them,

SELF-ESTEEM

Self-esteem refers to how an individual feels about him- or herself. Does someone view himself as a good person, worthy of good things? If he does, he probably has healthy self-esteem. If an individual views himself as flawed and unworthy of praise or the respect of others, he probably has low self-esteem.

Self-esteem motivates people's actions as well as the decisions they make. Individuals with positive self-esteem are likely to believe that they measure up to others sufficiently. They are more likely to have the confidence to pursue different accomplishments, whether it is trying to do well on a test, trying out for a sports team, answering a question in class, or applying for a job. These individuals are not overly afraid of failure; they realize that failure is a natural part of life and whether they fail or succeed at something does not indicate their overall worth and ability as a person.

People with low self-esteem, however, are less likely to try their best at anything. They are so certain they will fail that they approach tasks and challenges with so much anxiety (worry or fear) that they are unable to concentrate. They are so afraid of failure (which, in their eyes, will only serve to confirm their lack of worth and ability)

that they may not even try at all, finding it easier to believe that they may have succeeded had they really tried.

A strong sense of self and positive self-esteem can help prevent people from engaging in risky behavior or putting themselves in dangerous situations. These people know that, like all people, they deserve good things and that, regardless of one failure, success will come in the future in some way, shape, or form.

There are several factors that influence self-esteem. These include:

Age: Self-esteem tends to grow steadily up until middle school, which may be due to the transition of moving from the familiar environment of elementary school to a new setting with new demands. Self-esteem will either continue to grow after this period or begin to plummet.

Gender: Girls tend to be more susceptible to having low self-esteem than boys, perhaps because of increased social pressures that emphasize appearance rather than intelligence or athletic ability.

Socioeconomic status: Researchers have found that children from higher-income families usually have a better sense of self-esteem in the mid- to late-adolescence years.

people would not know where they came from, what they have experienced, or who their families and friends are. Memories are unique to each person. While many people may witness or experience the same event, each person will remember it differently. This is why memory is considered part of a person's complex personality.

Many scientists know what memory is, but they still don't know exactly how it works. Memory is defined as the ability to acquire information, store it, and then retrieve it later. It affects every aspect of people's daily lives. People have memories about facts, such as their names and phone numbers and birth dates. They also have memories about past events, such as graduation from high school, getting married, or the death of a loved one. In addition, memories of certain skills, such as how to talk, walk, cook, or play a sport exist in abundance. Still other memories seem to be instinctive. For example, people remember how to sleep, breathe, and digest food. These are just a few examples of what memory can do and how it helps people learn and live.

Different Kinds of Memory

Types of memory fall into two categories, or systems, in the brain. One system deals with fact knowledge, such as names and dates. The other system deals with skill. While scientists know these systems are separate, they think that the systems share with one another. What scientists do not know is how much they share and how closely they are connected.

Fact knowledge is usually referred to as short-term memory. Short-term memories can become long-term if the circumstances are right. Again, scientists are still unclear as to exactly how this works; however, they think that short-term memories do not last long because new information enters the part of the brain that stores short-term memories and then drives out older memories. If a short-term memory passes into the long-term memory, it has more staying power. It lasts longer and can eventually become permanent. The longer a memory lasts, the stronger it is and the less likely it will be forgotten. This happens because short-term memories are fragile, while long-term memories are sturdy. Some scientists believe that long-term memories are stored permanently because of chemical changes in the brain.

Other scientists do not categorize memories in terms of length. They believe that the length of a memory depends on certain circumstances; however, they do not know which circumstances produce long-term memories and which produce short-term memories. One thing scientists agree on, however, is the fact that the brain seems to have an unlimited capacity to store memories. Scientists continue to study how people store and retrieve memories and why, if they have an unlimited capacity to remember information, people forget.

How People Remember and Why People Forget

When memories are stored in the brain, they cannot serve people unless they are retrieved. How do people retrieve memories? This usually happens when memories are challenged. For example, if someone asks a question, a person must attempt to retrieve information in order to answer the question. Sometimes the answer is easy; other times, a person takes time to answer it. The amount of time it takes to answer the question is connected to a person's awareness of what memories are stored. Sometimes a person is not aware at the time that he or she knows the answer, but later realizes that the information is there, ready to be retrieved. Sometimes, a smell or a sound can trigger a memory that a person did not know was there.

Retrieving a memory involves finding the path that leads to the information and navigating that path. As more and more memories are stored from new experiences, those paths can become intertwined, making it more difficult to find the way back. It can become particularly difficult when stored information has similar meaning because a person will have trouble making distinctions between memories. For example, if a person has seen hundreds of movies, it may become difficult for the person to recall the details of each

THE POWER OF MEMORY

For unknown reasons, some people have a better ability to remember information than others. Ancient civilizations were able to maintain their history through an oral (spoken) tradition. Homer's epic poems *Iliad* and *Odyssey* were passed down through generations by word of mouth. It is believed that people's memories may have been stronger out of necessity. Because preliterate civilizations could not write, they were forced to remember things orally. When literacy (the ability to read or write) was developed, the need for oral stories diminished, which may explain why fewer people permanently store large amounts of information.

Some people have what is called eidetic imagery, or photographic memory, which enables them to take a picture of information and then use that picture to retrieve the information later. This picture is not just stored by sight. It can also be recorded through sound, taste, and smell. For example, a musician may be able to hear a song, and, without writing anything down, play back the song note for note. This type of memory is found more often in children than in adults. However, many people who have this ability as children often lose it as they grow older. Scientists do not know why some people have a photographic memory or why they eventually lose it.

There have been studies done, however, which reveal how too much memory can be harmful to a person. In the 1950s, a Russian man named Solomon V. Shereshevskii had the remarkable ability to remember an enormous amount of information. He was a reporter who was able to research and produce his stories without ever writing anything down. Shereshevskii eventually toured the world showing off his amazing ability to remember everything for an unlimited amount of time. Eventually, however, Shereshevskii's memory became an immense burden. Because he remembered so much information, he could not control his memories or when they surfaced. In the middle of conversations, he would be reminded of other events and facts until he could no longer concentrate on the conversation. He began to rant and rave like a madman. For the man who remembered everything, his greatest wish was to be able to forget.

one. The person may mix together certain parts or lines from different movies or may even confuse the actors involved in the movies.

Some people have trouble retrieving a memory, but eventually manage to do it. However, sometimes a memory cannot be retrieved at all. Does this mean that the information has disappeared forever? Scientists believe that as people search for a particular memory, such as the name of a childhood friend for example, they are actively retracing the path to find the original information that was stored years ago. If they make it there, the memory is retrieved. However, if people cannot seem to make it back on that path, they will never be able to find the memory. Sometimes, though, people will find their way by taking an alternate route. For example, if a person asks a friend a question, and the friend thinks he knows the answer but cannot seem to retrieve the information, he might say something like, "It's on the tip of my tongue!" Then, as he is doing something completely unrelated later in the day, the information might pop into his head. Scientists believe this happens because the brain has found a related item, which then helps the person find the desired information.

Ways to Improve Memory

Some scientists believe the capacity to store information long-term is connected to concentration. Short-term memories can easily become long-term if a person is willing to concentrate on the facts. Lynn Stern, author of *Improving Your Memory,* says that to make a long-term memory a person must "focus on it exclusively for a minimum of eight seconds." With training, anyone can improve the capacity to remember.

Experts also recommend the following to improve and maintain a good memory:

- Exercise on a regular basis. Exercise helps keep the blood flowing, which increases the amount of oxygen that reaches the brain. With more oxygen, the brain, and therefore the memory, stays sharp and focused.
- Manage stress. Stress can affect the body and the mind in negative ways. Emotional disorders such as depression can harm a person's ability to retrieve information.
- Stay organized. Organization creates order in a person's life. If a person is always losing her keys, her brain is being used to try to find them everyday instead of thinking about more important matters.
- Use visualization. Visualization means creating an image that corresponds with a fact or an event. If a person is trying to remember a list of groceries, it is helpful to associate a word, such as bread, with its corresponding image.
- Write it down. Writing things down on paper or on the computer helps people to remember because the act forces them to concentrate on the things they are writing. Concentration, as stated above, is one of the keys to a good memory.

Memory games are fun for young children, and also help develop important connections in the brain. (Photograph by Robert J. Huffman. Field Mark Publications. Reproduced by permission.)

LEARNING

When most people think of learning, they think of acquiring knowledge or a specific skill, such as facts about history, new vocabulary words, or how to play an instrument. Learning also encompasses behavior in a much broader sense than the aforementioned specifics. To mental health professionals, learning, on a most basic level, involves behavior modification. For example, when students learn how to do long math problems, they are using a process that a teacher showed them, but they are actually learning a behavior (how to solve long math problems). As a result, when presented with a math problem in the future, people draw on that behavior (or learned method) to solve the problem.

Of course, not everything that people do is learned through teaching or firsthand experience. Rather, there do exist some behaviors that are purely instinctual, or behaviors that people (and animals, too) are genetically programmed to exhibit in certain situations. An example of this is the fight-or-flight impulse. In a scary situation, the human body produces the steroid adrenaline, which makes the heart pump faster and the lungs work harder. This is an unconscious response that readies a person to "fight" if the situation calls for it or to "flee"; again, this is not a learned response to fear or danger but an instinctual one. These behaviors are also referred to as being innate responses (or inborn).

The Biology Behind Learning

When babies are born, their brains are made up of billions of neurons (nerve cells that carry messages to and from the brain to other parts of the body). Over time connections, called synapses, form among the neurons that are vital to proper brain functioning; these synapses help individuals make mental connections between different areas of the brain and between different information so that they may learn and develop to their fullest mental abilities. What drives the establishment of these synapses is stimulation, particularly during infancy and early childhood. Stimulation can be anything from color, to light, sound, or touch; anything that captures the child's attention and makes him or her think. When stimulation occurs, synapses are built and strengthened. Without stimulation or even reinforced stimulation, key synapses either will not form at all or will wither away. While things such as intelligence and creativity may be partially determined by heredity, these connections are what determine maximum development.

ALZHEIMER'S DISEASE

Alzheimer's disease is an illness that causes people to forget things, even the people in their lives. They cannot remember recent experiences they have had or how to perform tasks that previously required little or no thought at all. Alzheimer's usually afflicts people in their late sixties, seventies, and beyond; however, the disease has been diagnosed in people as young as thirty. The disease often progresses until a person has difficulty speaking or functioning on his or her own. Eventually, the body's basic functions, such as breathing and digesting, break down until the person enters a coma and dies. Sometimes the disease progresses quickly, and death results in as little as five or six years. Other times, a person suffers with the disease for as long as twenty years.

Alzheimer's is a devastating disease not only to the person afflicted but also to the family and friends who must witness their loved one's suffering. There are many organizations devoted to supporting families and friends who are dealing with the disease. In addition, scientists are working hard to discover new ways of coping with the disease and to develop new treatment.

Alzheimer's disease is difficult to diagnose. There are, however, some warning signs that help physicians determine if a person has Alzheimer's disease. The Alzheimer's Association of America has developed these ten warning signs. They are:

1. Memory loss that affects job skills. It is normal to occasionally forget an assignment, deadline or colleague's name, but frequent forgetfulness or unexplainable confusion at home or in the workplace may signal that something is wrong.

2. Difficulty performing familiar tasks. Busy people get distracted from time to time. For example, you might leave something on the stove too long or not remember to serve part of a meal. People with Alzheimer's might prepare a meal and not only forget to serve it, but also forget they made it.

3. Problems with language. Everyone has trouble finding the right word sometimes, but a person with Alzheimer's disease may forget simple words

What Helps Learning and What Hinders It

Stimulation, then, appears to hold an important key to making certain that people are able to realize their cognitive potential. Because the most important connections are made before the age of ten, it is important for a child to receive proper stimulation. There are several things that hold the key to optimizing learning and mental development for a child. They include:

1. A nurturing, secure environment that provides emotional caring and safety.

2. A sense of predictability so that a child develops a sense of emotional stability.

3. Conversation and communication; the spoken word boosts brainpower.

4. Encouragement and praise with regard to a child's accomplishments, however minor, to provide a sense of empowerment.

5. Helping children make cognitive connections by pointing them out (point out the car in the picture and then take the child for a ride in the car).

6. Knowing when a child has had enough stimulation and needs some quiet time.

or substitute inappropriate words, making his or her sentences difficult to understand.

4. Disorientation to time and place. It is normal to momentarily forget the day of the week or what you need from the store. But people with Alzheimer's disease can become lost on their own street, not knowing where they are, how they got there or how to get back home.

5. Poor or decreased judgment. Choosing not to bring a sweater or coat along on a chilly night is a common mistake. A person with Alzheimer's, however, may dress inappropriately in more noticeable ways, wearing a bathrobe to the store or several blouses on a hot day.

6. Problems with abstract thinking. Balancing a checkbook can be challenging for many people, but for someone with Alzheimer's, recognizing numbers or performing basic calculations may be impossible.

7. Misplacing things. Everyone temporarily misplaces a wallet or keys from time to time. A person with Alzheimer's disease may put these and other items in inappropriate places—such as an iron in the freezer, or a wristwatch in the sugar bowl—then not recall how they got there.

8. Changes in mood or behavior. Everyone experiences a broad range of emotions—it is part of being human. People with Alzheimer's tend to exhibit more rapid mood swings for no apparent reason.

9. Changes in personality. People's personalities may change somewhat as they age. But a person with Alzheimer's can change dramatically, either suddenly or over a period of time. Someone who is generally easygoing may become angry, suspicious or fearful.

10. Loss of initiative. It is normal to tire of housework, business activities, or social obligations, but most people retain or eventually regain their interest. The person with Alzheimer's disease may remain disinterested and uninvolved in many or all of his usual pursuits.

Reprinted with permission of the Alzheimer's Association of America.

Mental disorders such as attention-deficit disorder and learning disabilities can hinder learning, as discussed in Chapter 12 on Mental Illness. However, certain environmental factors and conditions can also hurt a child's ability to learn. A neglectful home environment in which stimulation is absent can spell the beginning of future learning problems for any child. Particularly stressful events, such as the death of a parent, or a stressful situation, such as homelessness, can also have adverse affects on a child's ability to concentrate on and respond to mental stimulation.

Kinds Of Learning

Several kinds of learning that are present throughout the life span influence the acquisition of knowledge and the alteration of behavior. Proposed by prominent doctors, scientists, and therapists throughout the years, their principles remain unchanged and are the foundation for many forms of therapies (for more information see Chapter 15: Mental Health Therapies).

CLASSICAL CONDITIONING. Formulated by Russian physiologist Ivan Pavlov (1849–1936), classical conditioning involves an automatic response to a certain stimulus that is acquired and reinforced through association. Pavlov illustrated the principles of classical conditioning after training dogs to salivate (involuntarily) upon hearing the ringing of a bell. Pavlov accomplished this task by first ringing a bell just before he fed the dogs. After a while, the dogs began to associate the ringing of the bell with getting their dinner. However, the response was ingrained in the dogs on such a deep level that the food was no longer the stimulus for salivation; rather, the ringing of the bell alone made the dogs salivate.

This can be seen in people's everyday behavior in different situations. An infant will learn to respond to the sound and smell of its mother before being given a bottle; the child is responding not to the bottle, but to the voice or scent of the mother. Similarly, if every time a child's parent calls him by his full name ("Come here, John Michael Smith!"), he gets yelled at, his heart may beat fast just hearing his full name being called, before his parent has even scolded him.

LET THERE BE LIGHT

Light and different types of light can influence and affect how one learns. In the 1940s and 1950s, biologist John Ott discovered that cool fluorescent lights (which are used in many classrooms) can make some children overly excited, thus making it difficult for them to learn, especially those students with attention-deficit disorder (see Chapter 12: Mental Illness). Natural light, or light that closely mimics natural light, is best for studying and learning.

OPERANT CONDITIONING. Unlike classical conditioning (which involves involuntary response to a certain stimuli), operant conditioning involves voluntary response to a certain stimuli based on positive or negative consequences that result from the response. First put forth by psychologist B.F. Skinner (1904–1990), an example of operant conditioning is training a dog by using treats or verbal praise to reinforce the desired result. If an owner trains her dog Fido to give her a paw when the dog's shoulder is touched and the dog performs the task and is rewarded with a biscuit or kind words, the dog will associate successfully performing the task with the tasty treat or the praise. Similarly, if a dog is consistently scolded when it chews something it should not, the dog will make the association between chewing a forbidden item with harsh words and will learn not to engage in that behavior anymore. The same principles apply to human behavior. If a child learns that she is rewarded by successfully completing her homework each night, doing her homework will become important to her.

Positive reinforcement of a behavior will usually cause a certain behavior to continue, while punishment or the absence of reinforcement will result in a behavior being extinguished. Behavior modification, a way of promoting positive behavior and eliminating negative behavior, is built around principles of operant conditioning.

OBSERVATIONAL LEARNING. Another way that people learn is through watching others or observing. A teacher trying to teach students how to add several numbers together will often explain the principles behind the method and will then demonstrate the method by solving a sample problem. The students then learn by observing the teacher. This is true of sports as well (watching a team execute certain plays during a sporting event) or behavior (watching someone get a desired result by giving a certain response). For example, a person might learn how to disarm her parents when they are angry with her by observing and adopting her brother's response, which seems to effectively calm their parents.

RIGHT-SIDE AND LEFT-SIDE DOMINANCE

There has been much attention given to the notion of brain dominance in recent years. A popular book on learning to draw is entitled *Drawing on the Right Side of the Brain: A Course in Enhancing Creativity and Artistic Confidence*. This refers to the split-brain theory put forth by scientists who believe that the left side and the right side of the brain represent different types of thinking and that each person leans toward one or the other.

The left side of the brain is geared toward verbal skills, analytical ability; the left side of the brain also emphasizes aggressiveness and rigid-ity, and organization. It has been found that left-brained individuals are typically drawn to pursuing careers as accountants, attorneys, or careers in the military. In contrast, the right side of the brain is more geared to artistry, playfulness, intuitiveness, and fluidity; passivity and emotional flexibility are signs of right-brain thinking. It has been found that right-brain people are more likely to become artists, entrepreneurs, and educators.

The theory of brain dominance, when applied to the arena of learning and education, means that instructors and parents, when possible, need to take into consideration whether a child is left-side or right-side oriented and tailor teaching methods to that dominance.

Young adults tend to observe the habits and behaviors of their peers, such as ways of dressing, and adopt them as their own. (Photograph by Robert J. Huffman. Field Mark Publications. Reproduced by permission.)

Observational learning is important in social learning. Young adults are likely to observe the habits and behaviors of their peers and adopt them as their own if they see those individuals gaining social acceptance through those habits and behaviors. This can include innocent things, such as ways of dressing or studying, or more harmful things, such as choosing to smoke, because those who do have gained a result that is desirable to those observing them.

Modeling (basing one's behavior on that of another person with whom there is a strong identification or desire to be like) is a part of observational learning, and young adults can model their friends' behavior as outlined in the previous paragraph. Modeling can also take place between people and someone they admire but do not personally know, such as a celebrity. For instance, if a young adult is a big fan of Madonna and hears that she does yoga every day, that young adult might be likely to take up yoga. The same holds true even if the person upon whom the teens are modeling themselves engages in harmful behavior. A celebrity who is caught engaging in risky behavior may influence young adults (and older adults) to engage in similar behaviors. Celebrities and public figures are often called "role models," even when they do not wish to be. They are generally held to higher standards than other people because their behavior is more likely to influence a large number of people.

INTELLIGENCE

Intelligence is defined most broadly as the ability and capacity to understand. It has taken many years for researchers to understand how to determine the precise differences between very intellectual individuals and those

LEARNING CAN BE FUN (AND GAMES)!

According to psychiatrist Gene Cohen (a game inventor, founder of the game company Genco, and former director of the National Institute of Mental Health's Center on Aging) games are mental gymnastics that can help people stay mentally fit. Cohen and other mental health professionals believe that playing games allows for people to flex brainpower and connections that they don't typically get to use when working or doing everyday tasks. Exercising the brain in this manner promotes the growth of better neural connections and the growth of brain cells.

Cohen's theories are backed up by research performed by Marian Diamond, a mental health professional at the Brain Research Institute of the University of California at Berkeley, who found that laboratory rats given toys to play with were able to find their way through mazes more quickly than rats who were not provided with toys. Upon examination of the two sets of rats the researchers discovered that there were profound differences in the brains of the two groups; the brains of the rats that had been given toys had more well-developed cerebral cortexes (which is the part of the brain related to thought). These findings gave rise to fun educational programs such as *Sesame Street*.

What Cohen wants people to remember, though, is that mental exertion through games can boost the brainpower of people—and rats as evidenced by Diamond's study—of all ages. Also, Diamond's study found that rats that simply watched other rats playing did not increase their brainpower at all. So, instead of passive activity such as watching television every night, to be mentally nimble in the years to come Cohen advises playing board games or cards. And, according to Cohen, computerized games do not boost brainpower because they do not involve reading nonverbal cues like watching one's opponents' reactions, which are part of traditional games.

who are less so. Until Alfred Binet (1857–1911), a French psychologist, sought to identify why certain students in French schools in the early twentieth century were not learning at the same pace as other students, no one had come up with any sort of solution to the question of how to measure intelligence. Using a trial-and-error approach to compiling his test, Binet developed his questions based on a division of students into categories of "bright" or "dull." The questions that ended up on the test were the ones that reinforced the difference in knowledge between these two groups.

The intelligence quotient (IQ) is the measure of intelligence as based on intelligence tests and the intelligence of the general population. While Binet created and published the very first standardized test of human intelligence (which was revised several times), it was American psychology professor Lewis Terman, of Stanford University, who came up with the actual formula for determining IQ: divide the test taker's "mental age," which is revealed by his or her score on the intelligence test, by his or her chronological age. The resulting number is what Terman called the intelligence quotient or IQ. In 1916 Terman brought the existing Binet test from France to the United States, translated it into English, and developed a new set of standard questions for American children. He named the new test Stanford-Binet.

In terms of how intelligent the general population is, the average IQ is 100, with 68.3 percent of people possessing IQs ranging between 85 and 115. People with IQs between 115 and 130 are classified as having superior IQs while those with IQs in excess of 130 are labeled as gifted. Those individuals whose IQ falls below 85 are labeled as borderline and any score under 70 often indicates that an individual is mentally impaired to some degree (see Chapter 12: Mental Illness for a discussion of mental retardation and its relationship to intelligence quotients).

DIFFERENT SMARTS FOR DIFFERENT PEOPLE

Many times, there are people who are not necessarily "book" or "school" smart but who are whizzes when it comes to specific fields such as music, art, or the written word. In response to this phenomenon, psychologist Howard Gardner came up with seven different types of intelligence. They include: musical intelligence; intelligence involving envisioning and measuring space abstractly (in one's mind, as artists and architects often do); mathematical intelligence; and linguistic intelligence (superior writing skills). In addition, there is interpersonal intelligence (being able to relate to others in a productive manner); intrapersonal intelligence (having the ability to be deeply in touch with oneself on an emotional and mental level); and physical intelligence (skills possessed by superior athletes, dancers, or surgeons).

Other theorists have brought forth issues of practical intelligence, or the intelligence that correlates with a person's success in day-to-day life. According to these theorists, practical intelligence, which comes from observing others, has a great deal of validity in that traditional intelligence does not have any correlation to success in life; often times, people with high IQs never realize their potential or lack the common sense to make the best of their capacities.

There are people who are not necessarily "book" or "school" smart but who are whizzes when it comes to specific fields such as music, art, or the written word. (Photograph by Robert J. Huffman. Field Mark Publications. Reproduced by permission.)

IQ tests have come to be viewed as predictors of a person's performance in school and in given careers. Over the years, however, the idea of intelligence, which is strongly tied to Binet's initial test, has come under fire. The notion of intelligence and ways of measuring it do not take into account that individuals with learning disorders, while still being very intelligent, may have trouble with the standard test. In addition, many people feel that intelligence tests are culturally biased (preferential to certain groups of people).

For example, the Stanford-Binet Intelligence Scale, which is based on Binet's initial test, includes questions for young children about "typical" daily activities. However, depending upon where one lives (for example, in the city or in the country, or in California or New York) or what one's experiences are, it might be difficult for some children to come up with the "correct" answer, according to the intelligence test, of what a typical daily activity is. In the case of adult testing, participants are asked to interpret the meaning of "common" proverbs (short sayings such as "A stitch in time saves nine"). It may be difficult to answer the question if a person has never heard of a certain proverb, or perhaps the proverb has a slightly different meaning depending on where a person grew up. Is it fair to say that someone possesses less intelligence than someone else because his or her life experiences do not coincide with the intelligence test?

Objectors to this type of intelligence testing propose that basic intelligence is not necessarily tied to knowledge, the acquiring of which has cultural biases. These concerns have given rise to a variety of intelligence tests that will measure not only verbal skills but also nonverbal skills and which are free of any bias.

CREATIVITY

Just as intelligence is difficult to explain in a precise manner, so is creativity. While intelligence refers to one's capacity to understand, creativity can be referred to as one's capacity to think in unique ways and solve problems in an imaginative manner. However, intelligence and creativity are not necessarily linked. People who are highly intelligent may not be very creative at all while extremely creative individuals may not have a particularly high IQ. Creativity can be demonstrated in endless ways, from creative writing to painting to architecture to simply performing any task in a creative manner, whether it is parenting, teaching, or building and repairing things.

Creative Thinking

Whatever a person's creative talent may be, the key to creativity lies in divergent thinking. Many people will respond to questions using convergent thinking (thinking that is driven by knowledge and logic). Divergent thinkers, however, will respond to queries with unusual but still appropriate answers. For example, if a convergent thinker were asked how many ways he could think of to use a book, he might respond with a conventional answer such as, "You can read it and learn from it." A divergent thinker also gives conventional answers such as those given by a convergent thinker. But he may be more creative and say, "You could pile books on top of each other to create a step stool, or you could use the book as a doorstop, or you could use it as a serving tray."

Creative individuals tend to share certain characteristics, including a tendency to be more impulsive (spontaneous) than others. Nonconformity (not going along with the majority) can also be a sign of creativity. Many creative individuals are naturally unafraid of experimenting with new things; furthermore, creative people are often less susceptible to peer pressure, perhaps

Coloring is one of the best ways for children to express their creativity. (Photograph by Robert J. Huffman. Field Mark Publications. Reproduced by permission.)

because they also tend to be self-reliant and unafraid to voice their true feelings even if they go against conventional wisdom.

How to Promote Creativity

In addition to taking some of the suggestions in the "The Creative Household" sidebar (see page 320), child development specialists suggest that there are other specific ways to promote creativity in children. Parents, guardians, and teachers should urge children to think divergently and come up with many different answers to a question or problem, answers that may fall outside of a traditional response, and should be careful not to ridicule an offbeat solution; rather, this sort of response should be taken seriously. Children should also be encouraged to be free thinkers who do not always accept things as they are but, rather, question what is and why it is. In this vein, too, kids should feel they have a right to examine things independently and not always accept the answer, "Because that's just the way things are."

Certainly, none of these things guarantees that a child or adult will necessarily be a creative person but it will help people to think creatively and to "color outside the lines."

FOR MORE INFORMATION

Books

Espeland, Pamela and Rosemary Wallner. *Making the Most of Today: Daily Readings for Young People on Self-Awareness, Creativity, and Self-Esteem.* Free Spirit Publishers, 1991.

Fogler, Janet and Lynn Stern. *Improving Your Memory: How to Remember What You're Starting to Forget.* Johns Hopkins University Press, 1994.

Gray, Heather M. and Samantha Phillips (illustrated by Ellen Forney). *Real Girl/Real World: Tools for Finding Your True Self.* Seal Press, 1998.

Palmer, Pat. *Teen Esteem: A Self-Direction Manual for Young Adults.* Impact Publishers, 1989.

Simmons, Cassandra Walker and Pamela Espeland. *Becoming Myself: True Stories About Learning from Life.* Free Spirit Publishers, 1994.

THE CREATIVE HOUSEHOLD

While no one is precisely sure why certain people are creative while others are not particularly so, researchers have been able to identify certain qualities that are often present in the upbringing and home environments of creative people. Parents and guardians of creative children have been found to have some things in common. Specifically, they are not very critical of their children and urge their children to pursue new activities and experiences. They also encourage openness and value creative thinking and curiosity; unusual questions and skills are also valued.

Another aspect these households share is that they are not overly strict in terms of having a lot of formal rules. There are a lot of family discussions and kids learn values and good behavior through these discussions and through modeling (see section on Learning). Adults in these households also try to give children access to lessons in different areas (dance, sports, music) and provide equipment to carry out these activities. Creative kids are also likely to collect certain things (dolls, trading cards), which is usually done with a parent's support. A strong sense of play and silliness was also present in the home.

Of course, creative individuals are raised in households of all kinds, and not just in environments such as described here.

Web sites

The National Association for Self-Esteem. [Online] http://www.self-esteem-nase.org/ (Accessed October 29, 1999).

Personality: What Makes Us Who We Are? [Online] http://www.learner.org/exhibits/personality (Accessed October 29, 1999).

12

Mental Illness

Mental, or psychological, illnesses and disorders occur in or relate to the mind. Mental disorders differ from physical (related to the body) disorders because there are usually no physical symptoms of a mental disorder (such as a broken arm or an upset stomach) for a doctor to observe. Mental disorders originate in the mind of an individual and display themselves outwardly through a person's behavior or emotions. When behavior or emotions are deemed "abnormal," a mental illness might be at the root of the problem.

In a world in which cultural and social differences are abundant, particularly as one moves from one country or region to another, it is very difficult to define what is "normal" behavior over what is "abnormal" behavior. However, abnormal behavior has come to be identified through the presence of different coexisting characteristics or conditions:

Infrequency is one facet of abnormal behavior; in other words, a behavior or characteristic exhibited or not exhibited by the majority of people determines normalcy. Another hallmark of abnormal behavior is whether or not the behavior violates social norms; this will differ from culture to culture and therefore allows for a range of differences in behavior. This can present difficulties in definition because while many criminals violate social norms, they are not always deemed to be mentally ill. Another way of identifying abnormal behavior is personal distress and the degree of an individual's suffering. For example, does a person's grief over something fall outside the scope of what is a "normal" level of grief or is it exceeding the average time it takes for an individual to recover from the grief?

Disability and dysfunction are also used to assess an individual's well-being. For example, someone with a great but irrational fear of something might not be able to participate in daily activities or may be experiencing a great deal of personal distress because of this fear. Finally, another factor in determining abnormality of behavior is whether someone's response to a situation is unexpected. For example, thirst is an expected response to not drinking enough fluids, but becoming emotionally distraught over thirst would not be an expected response.

Childhood Disorders

Mood Disorders

Psychotic Disorders

Anxiety Disorders

Other Types of Mental Disorders

This chapter describes a variety of major mental conditions and disorders. Some are deep-rooted mental illnesses, such as schizophrenia; others are more easily treatable, such as a learning disorder. Most mental disorders are treatable and, like many physical disorders, mental illness is not the result of something a person has or has not done to influence its development. Mental illness, like physical disease, can and does strike people from all walks of life. However, just as medical treatment for physical ailments has improved markedly over time, so has the diagnosis and treatment of mental illness.

CHILDHOOD DISORDERS

The classification of abnormal behavior in childhood depends greatly on development in terms of what is and is not considered normal behavior for a child at a certain age. This often makes it difficult to diagnose certain disorders of childhood as children develop at different rates and only a qualified therapist can make the distinction between what is appropriate and inappropriate behavior. Also, childhood disorders can be a sensitive subject,

WORDS TO KNOW

Adaptive behavior: Things a person does to adjust to new situations.

Affect: An individual's emotional response and demeanor.

Affectations: Artificial attitudes or behaviors.

Anhedonia: The inability to experience pleasure.

Antipsychotic drugs: Drugs that reduce psychotic behavior, often having negative long-term side-effects.

Anxiety: An abnormal and overwhelming sense of worry and fear that is often accompanied by physical reaction.

Attention-Deficit/Hyperactivity Disorder (ADHD): A disorder that involves difficulty in concentrating and overall inattentiveness.

Autism: A developmental disorder marked by the inability to relate socially to others and by severe withdrawal from reality. Language limitations and the extreme desire for things to remain the same are common symptoms.

Coexisting: Existing, or occurring, at the same time.

Compulsion: Habitual behaviors or mental acts an individual is driven to perform in order to reduce stress and anxiety brought on by obsessive thoughts.

Correlation: The relation of two or more things that is not naturally expected.

Delusions: False or irrational beliefs that an individual holds in spite of proof that his or her beliefs are untrue.

Depression: A disorder marked by constant feelings of sadness, emptiness, and irritability as well as a lack of pleasure in activities.

Down syndrome: A form of mental retardation due to an extra chromosome present at birth, often accompanied by physical characteristics, such as sloped eyes.

Dysfunction: The inability to function properly.

Dyslexia: A reading disorder that centers on difficulties with word recognition.

Empathy: Understanding of another's situation and feelings.

Enuresis: The inability to control one's bladder while sleeping at night; bed-wetting.

particularly learning disorders, as parents and children are afraid of the social stigma (shame) that often comes with a diagnosis. Children and adolescents strive for acceptance, and any indication of being different or being separated into "special" classes can have devastating effects on a child's self-esteem and the reaction of his or her peers to the situation.

The *Diagnostic and Statistical Manual of Mental Disorders* (DSM) and other sources categorize the following conditions as "Disorders Usually First Diagnosed in Infancy, Childhood, or Adolescence" or simply "Childhood Disorders"; technically, there isn't any difference between these disorders and other mental disorders except for the higher incidence of diagnosis in childhood rather than adulthood.

Attention-Deficit/Hyperactivity Disorder

Attention-deficit/hyperactivity disorder (ADHD) is a disorder that involves difficulty in concentrating and overall inattentiveness. ADHD affects

Genetic: Something present in the genes that is inherited from a person's biological parents.

Hallucinations: The perception of things when they aren't really present.

Humane: Marked by compassion or sympathy for other people or creatures.

Intelligence quotient (IQ): A standardized measure of a person's mental ability as compared to those in his or her age group.

Internalized: To incorporate something into one's self.

Irrational: Lacking reason or understanding.

Learning disorders: Developmental problems relating to speech, academic, or language skills that are not linked to a physical disorder or mental retardation.

Obsessions: Repeating thoughts, impulses, or mental images that are irrational and which an individual cannot control.

Phobia: A form of an anxiety disorder that involves intense and illogical fear of an object or situation.

Physiological: Relating to the functions and activities of life on a biological level.

Post-Traumatic Stress Disorder (PTSD): Reliving trauma and anxiety related to an event that occurred earlier.

Remorse: Ill feelings stemming from guilt over past actions.

Residential treatment: Treatment that takes place in a facility in which patients reside.

Savant: A person with extensive knowledge in a very specific area.

Schizophrenia: A chronic psychological disorder marked by scattered, disorganized thoughts, confusion, and delusions.

Social norms: Things that are standard practices for the larger part of society.

Somatogenesis: Having origins from within the body, as opposed to the mind.

Stressor: Something (for example, an event) that causes stress.

Suicide: Taking one's own life.

Tic: A quirk of behavior or speech that happens frequently.

Tourette's Disorder: A disorder marked by the presence of multiple motor tics and at least one vocal tic, as well as compulsions and hyperactivity.

people of all ages but is usually diagnosed in childhood. This condition has received a great deal of attention in the media in the last ten to fifteen years, because there has been a marked increase in the number of diagnoses of this disorder by mental health practitioners in recent years. No longer seen just as a problem centering around hyperactivity, or excessive activity, the focus of ADHD is also on a child's difficulty in concentrating on tasks at hand. While most children have notoriously short spans of attention, children battling ADHD have increased difficulty controlling their level of activity and attention particularly in situations that call for maintaining a certain degree of composure, such as in the classroom or in public places like restaurants.

ADHD makes it difficult for sufferers to sit still or even to stop talking. When they are called upon to be quiet and remain seated, they might squirm, fidget, tap their hands, swing their feet and legs, and make noise. The diagnosis is often difficult to make, as most children can be full of energy, particularly during times of play. However, children suffering from ADHD are disorganized, bossy and ill-mannered more often than the average child. Because of the increased prevalence of this diagnosis in recent years, there has

THE DSM, IV

Mental health care practitioners today rely heavily on the *Diagnostic and Statistical Manual of Mental Disorders, IV* (DSM, IV) to diagnose patients. Compiled and produced by the American Psychiatric Association, the DSM, IV is used by an array of individuals as well as by insurance companies. The DSM system of classification grew out of the *International Statistical Classification of Diseases, Injuries, and Causes of Death* or ICD, which was comprised of listings detailing all medical diseases and included abnormal behavior. The World Health Organization backed this system, but it was not widely accepted. In 1952, then, the first edition of the DSM was published, and it evolved into the comprehensive edition that it is today.

Controversy still exists around this volume, much of it based on the nature of categorizing mental illness in general. For example, the DSM, IV focuses largely on behavior while mental health researchers focus on psychological characteristics in assessing a condition. With each new edition of the DSM, efforts are being made to address all of these concerns; however, as society changes and new diagnoses are added, controversies will likely continue to arise.

The DSM, IV employs a multiaxial system of classification to rate an individual on five different levels. This is done to ensure that a wide array of possibilities and factors are considered when diagnosing a patient. Axis I includes all categories of mental disorders except personality disorders and mental retardation. These two categories comprise Axis II. Axis III covers medical conditions that are important to understanding a mental disorder, such as Alzheimer's disease. Axis IV includes problems or events that can affect the diagnosis, treatment, and outlook of a mental disorder (such as a death in the family, problems at work or school, and even issues such as living in an unsafe neighborhood). Axis V involves the use of the Global Assessment of Functioning (GAF) Scale, which mental health professionals use to assess how well an individual is functioning on a scale of 1 to 100. When used together, these axes are designed to allow a comprehensive diagnosis that takes into consideration all aspects of an individual's life and personality in making a diagnosis and implementing a treatment plan.

Attention-deficit disorder can make it difficult for some kids to concentrate in school. (Photograph by Robert J. Huffman. Field Mark Publications. Reproduced by permission.)

been the suggestion that children who are appropriately energetic, hard to handle, or suffering from a conduct disorder (see below) are being given a diagnosis of ADHD unnecessarily. This assessment, however, is difficult to quantify or prove. Furthermore, the Council on Scientific Affairs of the American Medical Association has investigated the issue and determined that while there isn't a concern for general overdiagnosis, some students belonging to minority groups are being diagnosed at a disproportionate rate.

SYMPTOMS. According to the DSM, IV some of the symptoms of ADHD include lack of attention to details; difficulty paying attention in school or at play; not paying attention when being spoken to; not following through on instructions or failure to finish things; disorganization, forgetfulness, losing or misplacing important things; fidgeting excessively; difficulty in playing quietly; excessive talking, difficulty in awaiting turn, and a tendency to interrupt others. In order to be diagnosed with ADHD, more than one of these symptoms must be present, and those symptoms must be creating a specific problem for the sufferer (lack of friends, poor performance in school, etc.).

CAUSES. Although there is no known single cause for ADHD, there are theories as to why certain children develop ADHD while others do not. Some experts propose that ADHD is inherited, while others have blamed the development of the disorder on environmental toxins, such as food additives or nicotine while a child is growing in the mother's womb. Psychological causes may include demanding, authoritative parenting that creates stress and triggers the development of ADHD.

TREATMENTS. ADHD has been treated effectively with certain drugs, including Ritalin, a stimulant that helps improve concentration, behavior, and directed activities. However, Ritalin's effectiveness has not been proven for the long term and some researchers have suggested that Ritalin actually hampers a child's creativity. Operant conditioning (see Chapter 15: Mental Health Therapies) has also been successful in helping those with ADHD. This therapy, which centers on rewarding good behavior, supports the belief that ADHD means that a child has a lack of basic skills to help him or her be effective, rather than the belief that a child simply has too much energy.

Conduct Disorder

Although conduct disorders cover a wide array of "bad" behaviors, the underlying principle of the diagnosis is that an individual exhibits inappropriate behaviors that violate the basic rights of other people. These are behaviors that fall outside the scope of normal childhood pranks and mischief; rather, conduct disorder includes behavior that is often vicious, and sufferers typically display no remorse (regret or guilt for having done something wrong), something that links conduct disorder to antisocial personality disorder or psychopathy (see section on Personality Disorders below).

In addition to the dysfunctional behaviors they exhibit, people with conduct disorders do not possess a great deal of empathy (understanding of other people's feelings) for others. Sufferers may also mistakenly think others are behaving aggressively toward them when they are not. Although an individual might seem to have a tough exterior, that person may in fact have low self-esteem, another feature common to those with conduct disorder. Recklessness, angry outbursts, and the tendency to get easily frustrated are also common traits of this problem.

SYMPTOMS. The DSM, IV splits conduct disorder into four categories: aggression toward people and animals (bullying, fighting, use of weapons, physical cruelty to both, stealing, and forced sexual contact); destruction of property (setting fires and destroying property deliberately through another method); deceitfulness or theft (breaking and entering, lying, covert stealing [e.g., forging a check]); and serious violations of rules (staying out past curfew at a young age, running away from home, and cutting school).

CAUSES. Just as with ADHD, there is no known single cause for conduct disorders, but there are theories as to why certain children develop conduct disorders while others do not. One theory is that conduct disorder may be an inherited ailment. Another possibility is that there is a lack of moral awareness in the family of origin of a person suffering from conduct disorder. In general, children learn what is right and wrong and refrain from breaking the boundaries of decency because they have been taught that it is wrong to hurt others. If, for whatever reason, these lessons are not learned in the home, a conduct disorder, and even more ominous psychological problems could develop. Furthermore, a child may witness disordered conduct from his or her parents and learn aggressive, improper behavior. Other researchers have postulated that children prone to developing conduct disorder could have flawed thinking processes. That is, very aggressive children may perceive an otherwise harmless event (for instance, being last in a line) as a slight, place unusual importance on the event, and hold a grudge because of the occurrence.

TREATMENTS. The most successful treatments of conduct disorders involve treating not just the child (or adult) but rather those around him or her as well (family and, in some cases, friends). Cognitive therapy, a form of therapy in which a therapist helps a patient become aware of maladaptive thinking and flawed belief systems and helps change beliefs that can interfere with healthy living (see Chapter 15: Mental Health Therapies), may also improve behavior as can teaching children moral reasoning skills.

Oppositional Defiant Disorder

Children often disobey their parents or teachers, particularly when they are extremely young, as a way of asserting their independence. However, when a child consistently is disobedient, disrespectful, hostile, and defiant toward parents, teachers, and other figures of authority for a period of six months, the child might be diagnosed with oppositional defiant disorder (ODD), a disorder that is not uncommon. Stubbornness and an unwillingness to deal rationally with others when there is disagreement are also signs of ODD.

Because defiant behavior is common in the development in both very young children and teenagers, it is cautioned that mental health practitioners make this diagnosis very carefully. Interestingly, more boys tend to suffer from ODD than girls do in the years before puberty; however, when adolescence arrives, both girls and boys are diagnosed at about the same rate.

The presence of this disorder is marked by a frequent loss of temper, arguing with adults, behaving annoyingly on purpose, blaming others for errors, anger, resentment, and spitefulness or vindictiveness. To be properly diagnosed with ODD, several of these characteristics must be noted for an extended period of time and these behaviors must prevent the child from performing properly at school or relating to family and friends.

While ODD may share similarities with both ADHD and conduct disorder, there are differences. Conduct disorder usually manifests itself in physical violence while ODD usually does not. ODD differs from ADHD in that the bratty behavior seen in ODD seems to be conscious and planned while

ADHD suffers seem unable to control their actions. Treatment for ODD often involves cognitive therapy and operant conditioning therapy featuring a system of rewards.

Learning Disorders

Learning disorders refer to developmental problems relating to speech, motor, and academic or language skills that are not linked to a physical disorder or mental retardation (see section below). The presence of a learning disability is not a reflection of how intelligent an individual is. In fact, people with learning disabilities are often of average or above-average intelligence, but there is a problem in development or processing that prevents that person from performing at proper levels. Most often, parents and teachers become aware of learning disorders through a child's results on standardized academic tests administered by the school. It is believed that learning disorders may be inherited, particularly dyslexia (see Reading Disorder below).

The treatment of learning disorders focuses on instruction in the area in which there are problems. The most effective programs are those that give children a chance to make small steps toward progress that can help restore self-esteem and confidence.

Learning disorders are broken down into three separate diagnoses: reading disorder, mathematics disorder, and disorder of written expression; there is also a generalized diagnosis (Learning disorder not otherwise specified) to address problems in all three areas or a combination of two areas.

READING DISORDER. A reading disorder is commonly known as dyslexia (pronounced dis-LEX-ee-a). Dyslexia comes from the Greek words "dys" (meaning poor or inadequate) and "lexis" (which refers to words or language). Dyslexia is a disorder that centers on difficulties with word recognition. Sufferers most often add, omit, or transpose (change the sequence of) letters in a word (for example, mistaking "sing" for "sign" or "left" for "felt"). All of these symptoms manifest themselves in problems with reading aloud, comprehending what is read, and spelling words correctly. Dyslexia can also affect mathematical skills, causing the person to add, omit, or transpose numbers.

MATHEMATICS DISORDER. While math can be difficult for many people, some children have difficulties that go beyond the normal scope. The problem can be as serious as someone being unable to recognize mathematical symbols and numbers to having difficulty following the proper steps in solving a mathematical equation. The degree of the difficulty is the key to making a diagnosis of mathematics disorder.

DISORDER OF WRITTEN EXPRESSION. This disorder centers on problems with writing skills. This, obviously, can affect many areas of academics, as can a reading disorder. Poor handwriting as well as difficulty with

Dyslexia is a learning disorder that centers on difficulties with word recognition. For example, "I surfed the net" can look like "I surfed the ten" to a sufferer of dyslexia. (Photograph by Robert J. Huffman. Field Mark Publications. Reproduced by permission.)

punctuation, grammar, and spelling are common. While many young people may have difficulties with some or all of these things, what makes a diagnosis necessary is the degree to which the problem interferes with academic achievement.

Mental Retardation

Mental retardation is a condition of below-normal mental ability or intelligence due to disease, injury, or genetic defect. The average person has an intelligence quotient (IQ) between 70 and 130, with the majority of the population having IQs between 85 and 115. (IQ is the measure of one's intelligence as based on intelligence tests and the intelligence of the general population; see Chapter 11: Mental Health for more information on IQ.) Those suffering from some degree of mental retardation have IQs below 70 and as low as 20. Accompanying a low level of intelligence is trouble with adaptive behavior or functioning (skills such as dressing oneself, being socially responsive, understanding certain abstract concepts like time and money, etc.). These conditions are usually discovered prior to the age of eighteen.

CAUSES. Often, there is no identifiable biological cause for mental retardation, especially in the cases of mildly or moderately mentally retarded in-

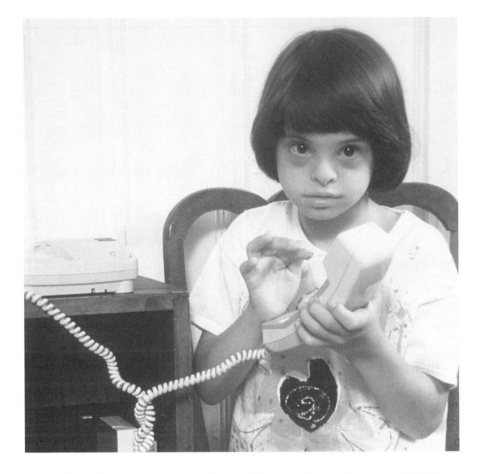

This child exhibits the outward physical signs of Down syndrome. (Photograph © 1996 Sean O'Brien. Custom Medical Stock Photo. Reproduced by permission.)

dividuals. However, in the cases of more severe mental retardation, genetic, or birth, defects—such as Down syndrome—can be the cause. Down syndrome usually causes people to have moderate to severe retardation. Furthermore, Down syndrome sufferers share certain physical characteristics that have become hallmarks of the disorder including oval, upward-slanting eyes; fine straight hair; and a stocky build and short stature. Other complications, including infectious diseases—such as encephalitis (swelling of the brain) and meningococcal meningitis (swelling of the lining around the brain or spinal cord)—can sometimes also cause mental retardation.

TREATMENTS. Treatment of mental retardation varies to the degree of retardation. Residential treatment, that is treatment in live-in residences, is very popular. Sometimes a patient will develop enough skills to move into a group home, which features a homey setting, living with patients at similar levels of functioning. Operant conditioning is often employed as well as certain cognitive therapies (see Chapter 15: Mental Health Therapies). Whatever the case, working with individuals to bring them to the highest level of functioning possible will benefit them; of course, compassion and protection are the key to helping these individuals lead comfortable, happy lives.

There are four major diagnoses relating directly to mental retardation:

MILD MENTAL RETARDATION. The IQ range for this diagnosis is between 50 and 55 to 70. Oftentimes, these individuals are not diagnosed as mentally retarded until later in their development because they are usually able to learn at a sixth-grade level. People who are mildly mentally retarded can usually hold jobs and often marry and successfully raise children. Approximately 85 percent of mentally retarded people have been diagnosed in this category.

MODERATE MENTAL RETARDATION. Ten percent of the mentally retarded are diagnosed with an IQ range of 35-40 to 50-55. Physical problems, including brain damage, are often present and tasks such as running or grasping things can be extremely difficult. Many people in this category live with their families or in supervised group homes with a great deal of success.

SEVERE MENTAL RETARDATION. Approximately three to four percent of individuals with mental retardation are at this level, with an IQ range of 20-25 to 35-40. Birth defects are often present and communication skills are limited. Although they may be able to do certain tasks under supervision, often they are unable to function independently in any capacity.

PROFOUND MENTAL RETARDATION. One to two percent of the mentally retarded have IQs falling below 20-25. These individuals require supervision for their entire lives. Because of physical deformities and other problems, people in this range often have a short life span.

Autism

Autism is a developmental disorder marked by the inability to relate socially to others and by severe withdrawal from reality. Language limitations and the extreme desire for things to remain constant are common traits of autism. Autistic children and adults seem to "look through" people and very often avoid eye contact. More often than not, they are unresponsive to touch and are unable to accept and display affection. An interest in ritual and repetitive body movements, such as rocking back and forth, and of repeating certain words or phrases, are also usually present. In many cases, speech is absent and, when it is

LIFE GOES ON

Life Goes On, a television program popular in the late 1980s and early 1990s, featured a main character, Corky, who was mentally retarded as a result of Down syndrome. Corky attended a mainstream public high school and even went on to marry. The character of Corky was portrayed by actor Chris Burke (1965–), who has Down syndrome in real life.

present, autistic individuals are often unable to hold a conversation with others. In some cases, those with autism may form strong attachments to inanimate (nonliving) objects, such as keys or even a refrigerator.

Another aspect of autism is that while many suffering from the disorder are mentally retarded to some degree (approximately 80 percent), they also may display almost incredible skill in other areas, such as mathematics. This facet of autism has prompted the use of the term idiot savant. A savant is one with detailed knowledge in a specialized field, such as math or science. Some people suffering from autism may also have exceptional memories or have a profound physical grace. Others with autism may, however, exhibit awkward physical affectations and posture and may not possess any outstanding, savant-like abilities.

Therapists work with a young autistic boy by using pet therapy (in this case a guinea pig) to help teach him how to relate to others. (Photograph © Helen B. Senisi. Photo Researchers, Inc. Reproduced by permission.)

CAUSES. Autism was originally thought to be the result of emotionally distant parenting but this has not been proven. However, a specific biological cause also has not been found. Still, it is believed that autism has its origins in biology, and studies of twins have indicated that autism may be genetic. It is difficult to confirm this, however, because of the rarity of autism (two to five births in 10,000) and the fact that persons with autism rarely have children. Most of the symptoms of autism are usually present and a diagnosis made by the time a child reaches toddler age.

TREATMENT. Treatment for autism is not always effective. However, operant conditioning and modeling (see Chapter 15: Mental Health Therapies) have proven to be successful in enabling parents to, at the very least, bring their child into social situations without the child acting out. Some therapists have had success in using intense behavioral therapy as well.

Tourette's Disorder

Usually diagnosed before a person reaches the age of eighteen, the main feature of Tourette's disorder is the presence of multiple motor tics and at least one vocal tic (a tic is a quirk of behavior or speech that happens frequently). Examples of such tics include frequent eye blinking, throat clearing, sniffing, repeating words or sounds over and over, or coprolalia (repeatedly saying obscenities). Such symptoms must be exhibited for more than a year, without a lapse in symptoms exceeding three months in a row, and

THE TEMPLE GRANDIN STORY

There are those with autism who have managed to become fully functional adults. One woman, Temple Grandin, Ph.D., was diagnosed with autism at the age of three. Her case has been documented by neurologist Dr. Oliver Sacks, and she has written two autobiographical books. Grandin managed to learn how to speak by age six and went on to earn her doctoral degree in animal science, to run her own business, and instruct courses at Colorado State University. However, for all of her academic and professional achievements, she still remains in awe of people and human relations, calling herself an "observer" rather than a participant in the social realm of life. While she has managed to overcome many of the negative traits of autism, such as violent rages and acting out impulsively and seemingly without reason, she has been unable to bridge the gap between herself and others on an emotional level. Dr. Sacks noted that while Grandin is able to converse at length about intellectual matters, she lacks many standard social graces (manners).

the condition must have a negative effect on one area of functioning (social, educational, professional, etc.). More common in males than females, the average onset age of Tourette's is seven.

SYMPTOMS. Symptoms accompanying Tourette's range from obsessions and compulsions (see section on Anxiety Disorders below), to hyperactivity, social discomfort, and depression. Social problems and depression may stem from embarrassment over a sufferer's inability to control his or her actions. Exaggerated behaviors not uncommon to Tourette's, such as head banging, knee bending, head jerking, and picking the skin, can cause injury and/or illness.

CAUSES. Tourette's disorder is genetic in origin. While not all individuals who inherit the predisposition toward Tourette's will develop the disorder, 70 percent of females and 99 percent of men carrying the genes will develop it.

TREATMENTS. Tourette's is often treated with prescription drugs, which can help to lessen the presence of tics and other symptoms.

Stuttering

Many people have heard another person stutter; what might strike many people is the number of individuals who have outgrown or overcome stuttering. Stuttering is a disturbance in verbal fluency of speech; for example, a stutterer might repeat whole words several times before being able to move on to the next word in the sentence ("I want to go-go-go-go to the movies."). Another sign may be a person's consistent difficulty in pronouncing certain consonants, or having long pauses between words in a sentence.

WHEN A STUTTERER SINGS, HIS STUTTER EITHER IMPROVES MARKEDLY OR DISAPPEARS. THIS MAY HAVE TO DO WITH BREATHING, BEING RELAXED, AND A STUTTERER KNOWING EXACTLY WHAT HE IS GOING TO SAY (STUTTERERS OFTEN STUTTER LESS WHEN READING ALOUD).

Stuttering is frustrating because, like Tourette's, it separates people from others by hampering easy communication. It can also affect learning, as a child may be embarrassed to ask or answer questions in class because of fear of classmates' teasing. Furthermore, stuttering can become worse when one is nervous, which can prevent a stutterer from answering difficult questions or doing any type of public speaking.

Stuttering affects more males than females and usually is present at or around the age of five. It has been estimated in the DSM, IV that eighty percent of stutterers recover, with sixty percent overcoming their stutter through no apparent reason. Speech-language pathologists (see Chapter 7: Health Care Careers) perform therapy with stutterers to help them overcome the disorder.

MOOD DISORDERS

Mood disorders cause a disturbance in mood (state of mind) and include depression and bipolar disorders. Mood disorders can be devastating as, depending on their severity, they can emotionally paralyze people, rendering them unable to work or attend classes or even enjoy the most basic things. Mood disorders can also disrupt appetite and sleep patterns and an individual's sense of well-being. It is not known why some people suffer from mood disorders while others do not.

Major Depression

Major depression, the condition of feeling deep and constant sadness, is one of the most common mental disorders. It strikes almost one in five people at some point. More common in women than in men, depression tends to recur, making it a lifelong battle for some people. Depression, too, has become more common over the last few decades. This may be attributable to social changes that have occurred simultaneously (society moving at a faster pace, individuals bearing more stress as life becomes increasingly urbanized, and many institutions—church, family, cultural customs—that once acted as support systems no longer as common). It may also be that people are more aware of the symptoms of depression and are more willing to seek treatment than in the past.

BED-WETTING

For many children, nighttime enuresis, or bed-wetting, is an embarrassing and painful problem. The inability to control one's bladder while sleeping is stressful and, unfortunately, still something of a mystery. Enuresis will not be diagnosed until after a child is at least five years old (the age by which most children have been toilet-trained). At age five, the DSM estimates that approximately seven percent of boys and three percent of girls are enuretic. Furthermore, the majority of enuretics have always had problems with bladder control during the night (they are called primary enuretics); secondary enuretics, in the minority, were once able to control their bladders but have lost that ability.

A variety of factors have been blamed for bed-wetting. There is a strong genetic link for bed-wetting (if a parent wet the bed, the child is much more likely to do so). Certain medical conditions cause enuresis, such as urinary tract infections and kidney disease. Some psychoanalytic therapists have suggested that bed-wetting is an act that can indicate anger toward parents. Still other schools of therapists have proposed that children encounter enuresis when they have been toilet-trained at too early an age.

Whatever the cause, enuresis is treatable. Using principles of classical conditioning (see Chapter 15: Mental Health Therapies), Drs. O.H. Mowrer and W.M Mowrer developed the bell-and-pad apparatus, which involves a pad that, when moisture hits it, sounds a bell, waking the child and prompting him to go to the bathroom to finish urinating. Prescription medicine is also effective in ending episodes of bed-wetting but is only effective when it is being used; when enuretics stop taking the drugs, the bed-wetting returns. Many enuretics simply outgrow the problem as they approach puberty.

SYMPTOMS. There are several possible symptoms of depression, whether it be a major depressive episode (which lasts approximately up to two weeks) or major depressive disorder (of longer duration and higher rate of return of the depression). Symptoms can include: constant feelings of sadness, emptiness, or irritability; a lack of pleasure in activities, even those that once brought enormous pleasure; a noticeable drop or increase in weight; the inability to sleep; extreme exhaustion; feelings of worthlessness; an inability to make decisions or concentrate on performing tasks; and thoughts of death and suicide. In order for a diagnosis of depression to be made, none of these symptoms can be caused by drugs or a medical disorder (there are separate categories of depression that are caused by illness or substance abuse) and a diagnosis should not be made if an individual is mourning the very recent loss of a loved one.

CAUSES. Many different theories account for the development of depression, depending upon the therapist's school of thought. Psychoanalysts (see Chapter 15: Mental Health Therapies) believe that the seeds of depression are sown in early childhood when something goes wrong with one stage of development or another. Cognitive therapists, such as Aaron Beck, believe that an individual battling depression has a faulty perception of the world, tending to view things negatively, and this impacts the person and his or her

Mood disorders can make a person unable to enjoy the company of others, which brings on feelings of isolation. (Photograph by Robert J. Huffman. Field Mark Publications. Reproduced by permission.)

A diagnosis of major depression should not be made if a person is mourning the recent death of a loved one, which is perfectly normal. (Photograph by Robert J. Huffman. Field Mark Publications. Reproduced by permission.)

reactions to different situations later in life, increasing susceptibility to developing depression. Behavioral therapists believe that depression may strike individuals who do not have strong social support and whose depression further deepens their isolation from others. There are also those who attribute depression to biological causes, including the possibility that it is inherited or caused by a chemical imbalance in the brain.

TREATMENTS. Depression has been treated with success with cognitive therapy and interpersonal therapy (a therapy that focuses on how a person interacts with others and which instructs him or her how to interact more

Kurt Cobain, lead singer of the band Nirvana, committed suicide in 1994 while at the peak of a successful career. (Photograph © Ken Settle. Reproduced by permission.)

effectively). Drug therapies have also worked well in treating depression. Antidepressants, such as Tofranil and Elavil, as well as Prozac, have been effective in alleviating the symptoms of depression. Drug therapies are most beneficial when they are accompanied by sessions with a therapist who can help an individual better understand depression and how he or she is reacting to the medication.

Bipolar Disorder

Bipolar disorders are marked by extreme highs and extreme lows in mood. Similar to depression in that they include the occurrence of major depressive episodes, bipolar disorders are also accompanied by manic episodes or hypomanic episodes. A manic episode is when a person is in an intense emotional state of elation (extreme happiness) and overactivity in which he or she is abnormally energetic and talks in an almost stream-of-consciousness way, with ideas and grandiose plans being shared (however implausible they may seem). Examples of other symptoms of a manic episode include an inflated sense of self, a reduced need for sleep, and engaging in reckless activities (for example, irresponsible sexual behavior or excessive spending). A hypomanic episode is similar to a manic episode though not as extreme.

Bipolar I disorder is marked by manic episodes accompanied by major depressive episodes. Bipolar II disorder has major depressive episodes at its center which are accompanied by at least one hypomanic episode.

Bipolar depression also differs from major depression, which is also known as unipolar depression, in that it strikes males and females at the same rate. Typically, bipolar depression is treated with drugs and counseling. As with major depression, there exists a genetic correlation.

PSYCHOTIC DISORDERS

Psychotic disorders, including schizophrenia, center around psychoses, which refer to mental disorders that involve a dramatic impairment in think-

SUICIDE: A DEADLY SIDE-EFFECT OF DEPRESSION

Suicide is when a person takes his or her own life. Not all people who kill themselves do so solely because of depression. However, many depressed people entertain the thought of ending their lives, attempt to end their lives, or sadly, succeed in ending their lives. Often times, the first sign of a person's depression may be a suicide attempt.

According to the American Psychiatric Association, depression is very common among teenagers and young adults. Studies have shown that teens who are depressed, abusing substances, or acting out on violent feelings are all at high risk for suicide. In fact, among teens and young adults between the ages of 15 and 24, suicide is the third leading cause of death. It is estimated that 5,000 teens commit suicide each year.

Suicide prevention centers around the country offer twenty-four-hour assistance to people in despair and considering suicide. However, the most important mechanism in preventing suicide can usually come from the depressed or despondent person or the people around that individual. Watching for warning signs of depression or reckless behavior and helping someone get professional counseling is crucial in preventing this senseless act. These warning signs can include: sleep disturbances (sleeping too much or too little), a change in appetite and weight, feelings of restlessness, lack of concentration, withdrawal from friends and activities once considered fun, sudden mood swings, and feelings of guilt and hopelessness.

ing, such that an individual is almost completely out of contact with reality. Most often this means that a person is experiencing hallucinations, or having delusions. Hallucinations are the perception of things that aren't present (seeing things, hearing things, etc.); delusions are false or irrational beliefs that an individual holds in spite of proof that those beliefs are untrue. It is these qualities that render psychotic disorders frightening and mysterious, especially for those afflicted by them.

Schizophrenia

Schizophrenia, perhaps the most severe psychotic disorder, is still not fully understood by the mental health community. When it strikes, more often than not, sufferers need to be on medication for the rest of their lives in order to keep the disorder under control. Furthermore, many schizophrenics are unable to resume normal lives; this tragedy is compounded by the fact that schizophrenia often develops when individuals are in their late teens through mid-thirties. This means that some persons could have been working toward building a full life only to find themselves in jeopardy of losing everything they have worked for.

SYMPTOMS. Symptoms of schizophrenia include having scattered, disorganized thoughts. People with schizophrenia will lose their train of thought when conversing with others, often bringing up completely different issues and causing others to become confused. Delusions are another symptom of schizophrenia. Delusions can include anything from a person's belief that others are plotting against him or her, or that a person's food is being poisoned because someone is trying to kill him or that another person can read his mind. Hallucinations often accompany delusions as well. Many times, schizophrenics hear strange voices inside their heads. Naturally, this is extremely disturbing and feeds a schizophrenic's fear.

Other symptoms include a lack of motivation to engage in normal daily activities, such as maintaining one's hygiene or doing chores. Also, although schizophrenics will tend to speak, they will have less to say; their conversations may be repetitive and nonsensical. The inability to experience pleasure, known as anhedonia, may also be present, as may problems with a person's affect (an individual's emotional response and demeanor); often times, a schizophrenic's affect may be flat (lacking in emotional response) or inappropriate (for example, laughing upon hearing that someone has died).

CAUSES. There is no single, definitive answer as to why some people develop schizophrenia. It is believed that it is genetic and that if a person has a schizophrenic relative in his or her family, there is an increased incidence of the person developing schizophrenia. Studies on families and twins have supported the genetic link, although the statistics are not very high, meaning that there may be schizophrenia in a family's gene pool, but the likelihood of someone developing it isn't all that great. Among twins with schizophrenia, the incidence of both having the disorder is quite high in identical twins (almost 44.30 percent according to one 1987 study); further, fraternal (nonidentical) twins also have an increased risk, although it's not as high as in identical twins.

It has also been suggested that chemical imbalances in the brain could account for the development of schizophrenia, something that certain researchers believe may also be inherited as well. Finally, psychological stress has been identified as being a possible cause.

TREATMENTS. Schizophrenia is almost always treated with antipsychotic drugs, such as Thorazine, which reduce psychotic symptoms, particularly because hallucinations and delusions can cause schizophrenics to engage in behaviors that make them a risk to themselves and even others around them. Medication is usually successful in suppressing symptoms but, alone, it is not enough. Therapy is a necessary ingredient in treatment to help the individuals accept and cope with their situations and understand the importance of continuing to take medication even if they feel "cured." Therapy can also be useful in helping a schizophrenic's family understand the patient's plight and contribute to helping manage and maintain a person's plan of care.

ANXIETY DISORDERS

Anxiety, the unpleasant feeling of fear and apprehension, is something that most people experience at one point or another in their lives. People have anxious feelings about taking tests, speaking in public, interacting with the opposite sex, making new friends and acquaintances, traveling to strange places, or personal situations (for example, money, job, family, etc.). Anxiety of this nature is completely normal, as long it does not prevent people from going ahead and doing these activities anyway, facing their minor fears or worries and moving forward.

Sometimes, though, some people find that they are paralyzed by their anxiety about a situation or a thing and cannot act. Instead of doing what they know they should, they retreat and avoid the situation entirely. This might not seem too harmful if it is a case of a person being afraid, for example, of tigers. As long as he or she doesn't live in an area populated by such animals, the situation might never present a problem. However, what happens if individuals have extreme anxiety in social situations to the point that they avoid interacting with others entirely? Or, what if people are so afraid of germs that they cannot stop compulsively cleaning themselves to the point that they are unable to engage in normal activities for fear of contamination? It is at this point that individuals must seek professional help in order to conquer their fears so that they can live normal, full lives.

Phobias

Phobia is a form of an anxiety disorder that involves intense and illogical fear of an object or situation. Usually, the individual is aware that the fear is out of proportion to the danger of the thing they fear. In other words, someone being afraid of skydiving or rock climbing wouldn't have a phobia; both of these activities carry high risks for injury or death. However, someone who has never had a negative experience with a dog but is afraid of dogs has a phobia. And, even allowing for the fact that a person has had a negative experience with the thing or situation feared, the presence of a phobia is indicated if the level of fear is out of proportion with the threat the situation or object presents.

The most common phobia is agoraphobia, the fear of public places. This is a phobia that can impair a person's ability to connect with others, to at-

Don't look down! The fear of heights, called acrophobia, is a common phobia. (Photograph by Robert J. Huffman. Field Mark Publications. Reproduced by permission.)

tend school, and to hold a job. People with severe agoraphobia will not only avoid crowds and busy places, some may refuse to leave their homes entirely. Other common phobias include the fear of heights, called acrophobia, and claustrophobia, which is the fear of closed spaces (such as elevators or overly crowded rooms that leave little personal space).

TREATMENTS. Treatments for phobias usually involve confronting the fear in some way. Behavioral therapists (see Chapter 15: Mental Health Therapies) may use a variety of techniques that involve visualization or actual contact with the object or situation around which the phobia centers. The thinking behind this, for certain schools of therapies, is that it will desensitize the phobic to the phobia. For example, flooding, a behavioral technique, involves exposing a phobic person to the cause of the phobia in an extreme way; however, this can cause the phobic serious initial discomfort, at the very least, and many therapists shy away from therapies that could potentially traumatize a patient.

Operant conditioning is also used in similar ways. Cognitive therapists will work with phobics using cognitive therapies alone (without some type of exposure to the source of the phobia), but this is usually effective only in the case of social phobics. Furthermore, social phobics have responded well to behavioral techniques that involve acquiring better social skills so that they feel more comfortable in social situations. Drugs have also been used to lessen a phobic's anxiety but drugs only mask the fear and will not solve the problem in the long term.

Panic Attacks and Disorder

A panic attack can accompany several different anxiety disorders, so in and of itself, a panic attack is not a separate disorder. Essentially, a panic attack is a short period involving intense feelings of fear or discomfort along with several telltale symptoms. These symptoms include an irregular or accelerated heart rate or a pounding of the heart; sweating, discomfort or pain in the chest; a feeling of choking or not being able to breathe properly; trembling, feelings

WHAT ARE YOU AFRAID OF?

For every fear, it seems there is a phobia. Listed below are just some phobias, from the common to the plain weird.

Phobia	Meaning
Ailurophobia	The fear of cats
Bibliophobia	The fear of books
Coulrophobia	The fear of clowns
Didaskaleinophobia	The fear of going to school
Entomophobia	The fear of insects
Glossophobia	The fear of speaking
Heliophobia	The fear of the sun
Ichthyophobia	The fear of fish
Lachanophobia	The fear of vegetables
Myctophobia	The fear of darkness
Nosocomephobia	The fear of hospitals
Ophidiaphobia	The fear of snakes
Pantophobia	The fear of everything
Rupophobia	The fear of dirt
Sophophobia	The fear of learning
Triskadekaphobia	The fear of the number 13
Urophobia	The fear of urine or urinating
Xenophobia	The fear of strangers or foreigners
Zoophobia	The fear of animals

of detachment, of things being "unreal," and/or of impending doom. People experiencing panic attacks have described feeling as though they would lose control completely or were about to have a heart attack or stroke.

Panic attacks can be caused by certain situations, such as being in a strange place, or while a person is relaxing or even sleeping. If panic attacks continue to occur when there is no apparent stressor (stress-inducing event), an individual might be diagnosed with having panic disorder. Panic disorder is a reasonably common ailment, affecting two percent of men and five percent of women. It may begin in adolescence and the disorder is inherited. Biological theories as to the disorder's origin have been put forth as have theories that suggest that panic disorders and agoraphobia are solely psychological in origin. Furthermore, one set of researchers has even suggested that the agoraphobia that so often coexists with panic disorders isn't really a fear of public places but rather a fear of losing control and having a panic attack in a public place.

Certain drugs, such as antidepressants, have been used to treat people with panic disorder and agoraphobia with some success; however, the drugs are merely a temporary measure as people's symptoms will return when they stop taking the drugs. A better approach in terms of a cure might be methods used by cognitive and behavioral therapists, which have proven to help lessen the severity of the disorder.

Obsessive-Compulsive Disorder

Obsessive-compulsive disorder (OCD) involves obsessions (repeating thoughts, impulses, or mental images that are irrational and which an individual cannot control) and compulsions (habitual behaviors or mental acts an individual is driven to perform in order to reduce stress and anxiety brought on by obsessive thoughts or because individuals believe those behaviors or acts will prevent a certain calamity from occurring [for example, believing that a certain behavior will prevent a car accident]). While almost every person may have behavioral quirks or strong preferences (cracking one's knuckles, or wanting things to be kept neat), obsessions and compulsions are different in that they prevent people from living normal lives because they take up an inordinate amount of time.

Obsessions can include thoughts ranging from a person constantly thinking about becoming "contaminated" with germs and avoiding shaking hands with others because of that fear, to a person being convinced that he has left his front door unlocked. The compulsions accompanying these obsessions can include things such as someone repeatedly washing hands for fear of germs, or checking repeatedly (sometimes a certain number—for instance, three times) to see if they have indeed locked the front door. Unlike preferences, a compulsion is something that is viewed as not being part of someone's personality but rather irrational behavior that a person is unable to stop.

Due to the nature of this disorder, it can separate people from others, rendering afflicted individuals unable to participate in everyday activities because their obsessions and compulsions prevent them from doing so.

CAUSES. There are many theories surrounding the development of OCD. Behavioral and cognitive therapists believe that the behaviors and thinking related to OCD are learned and reinforced. For example, a person may have the irrational belief that she has not locked her door; by going back to check whether or not it is indeed locked, she is able to relieve the stress that is related to her worries. Some therapists have also pointed to the fact that a lot of the problem stems from the fact that those suffering from OCD simply cannot remember whether or not they did something. There can also be organic (relating to the body) causes for OCD, such as head injuries and brain tumors as well as chemical imbalances in the brain.

TREATMENTS. Treating OCD is not an easy task. One of the most successful therapies involves placing a person in a situation that usually triggers his anxiety, but the patient is not allowed to engage in the compulsive behavior that is the typical response. The idea is that eventually the stress from not performing the compulsive behavior will lessen over time to the point where the person no longer feels compelled to do it.

Prescription drugs have also proven successful in reducing a person's obsessive thoughts and compulsive behaviors; this approach will not necessarily resolve the problem entirely but will free a person to live a normal life while confronting the issues appropriately through therapy.

Post-Traumatic Stress Disorder

Every day, people experience traumatic events, anything from being in a car accident to being robbed or even witnessing such an event happening to someone else. While people may survive these events (which involve intense fear and a feeling of helplessness), and their physical wounds may heal, they can still carry emotional scars. When an individual experiences emotional aftereffects from a traumatic event days, months, or even years after the actual event, this is known as post-traumatic stress disorder (the prefix "post" means after or later). Many of these individuals, even much later, will relive the event, become extremely upset and/or have nightmares about the event. They will also try to avoid things that remind them of the trauma. Finally, they may also be plagued by sleep disruptions, have difficulty concentrating, and startle easily and dramatically.

Post-traumatic stress disorder received a great deal of attention in the years following the Vietnam War (1954–75), as it had after World Wars I (1914–17) and II (1939–45), the Korean Conflict (1950–53) and, in fact, even after earlier conflicts such as the American Civil War (1861–65), because of the emotional scars that those who had served in a war often seemed

Post-traumatic stress disorder affected many students (pictured at a memorial service) and adults alike after the 1999 Columbine High School shootings in Littleton, Colorado. (Photograph by David Zalubowski. AP/Wide World Photos. Reproduced by permission.)

to display. In fact, PTSD was originally called "shell shock" (in reference to the ammunition used during times of war). It is now known that those who have witnessed or participated in any type of traumatic event—such as being involved in the search-and-rescue or recovery missions for the victims of plane crashes in which hundreds of people perish—are now known to be potential sufferers from PTSD. What is mysterious about PTSD is why it affects only certain people and not all of those experiencing similar events or even the same event.

TREATMENTS. Great strides have been made in treating PTSD through group therapy. Talking in a group to others who have experienced similar events and have been suffering from them continuously can be very helpful because patients can feel that they are not alone in their feelings and that there are people who understand the intensity of their traumatic experience. Most therapies, in groups or single client therapy, usually will involve confronting the event in some way. Stress management and medication have also been used with some success.

People who have lived through traumatic events should be encouraged to seek at least brief therapy to ensure that PTSD won't develop years later.

OTHER TYPES OF MENTAL DISORDERS

There are a number of other mental or psychological disorders that afflict millions of people each day. These can range from disorders most often appearing in old age, such as Alzheimer's disease, to gender-identity disorders, in which people wish to be members of the opposite sex. Eating disorders are also a common mental illness. [For more information on eating disorders, see Chapter 13: Eating Disorders.]

What follows is a small sampling of other common psychological disorders.

Somatoform Disorder

Sometimes people will complain of pain or discomfort that lingers but, when these individuals seek medical treatment, doctors can find no physical cause for the symptoms. When this persists, and the pain and discomfort prevent a person from participating in day-to-day life, a mental health professional may diagnose that person with pain disorder, which is just one of several somatoform disorders. Somatoform disorders are psychological disorders that manifest themselves physically without the presence of a true physical ailment.

Somatoform disorders can include conversion disorders, which can result in sudden loss of vision (once called hysterical blindness) or paralysis. People have also been known to lose their senses of hearing and smell as well. Another somatoform disorder is body dysmorphic disorder (BDD). While many people would like to change something about themselves (such as being more muscular, having smaller ears, having straight or curly hair, being taller or shorter, etc.), people with BDD grossly exaggerate what they perceive to be flaws with themselves and spend hours obsessing about these so-called flaws. Some BDD sufferers even take measures to act upon their impulses by picking at their skin (if they think they have too many blemishes) or getting plastic surgery unnecessarily.

As with many other mental disorders, there is no single theory that can account for why certain people develop somatoform disorders while others do not. Oftentimes, a person will recover suddenly from the problem while others require therapy. Behavior therapists will use techniques that center around making it appealing for a person to abandon his or her symptoms. Other therapists have used techniques similar to those used on people with phobias, wherein the patient will be exposed to the cause of the stress in order to diminish its effect.

Dissociative Disorder

When someone dissociates, it means that a certain behavior or part of the personality becomes removed from the rest of his or her consciousness. This can be something as harmless as becoming preoccupied while listening to a song on a portable stereo while walking and then not remembering which route was taken upon arriving at a destination. However, dissociation can also be a very serious problem and several disorders are attached to this phenomenon.

DISSOCIATIVE AMNESIA. Dissociative amnesia, which occurs when a person cannot remember personal information, such as where a person has

BARON VON MUNCHAUSEN AND MENTAL ILLNESS

Baron Von Munchausen was an eighteenth-century German huntsman and soldier known for telling greatly exaggerated tales about his exploits. Because of his reputation and the publication of tales based on his anecdotes (written by Rudolph Erich Raspe), the name Munchausen is now associated with exaggeration. So it came to be that when people faked symptoms of illnesses or parents faked the illnesses of their children, those disorders were named the Munchausen syndrome and Munchausen-by-proxy syndrome, respectively.

Although Munchausen syndrome and Munchausen-by-proxy syndrome are still recognizable names and in use, the proper clinical terms for these somatoform disorders are malingering (in the case of an individual who fakes illness in order to avoid doing something or to receive at-

tention) and factitious disorder (in which a parent or guardian lies about a child's medical history and current condition in order to make others believe the child is ill). Both syndromes go beyond fibbing; they are serious psychological disorders, and both have consequences that affect others.

In the case of malingering (or Munchausen syndrome), a healthy individual is wasting the time of medical professionals and perhaps even taking up valuable bed space in a hospital. Factitious disorder (or Munchausen-by-proxy syndrome) can threaten the life of an otherwise healthy child because the disturbed caretaker may even go so far as to injure the child or taint blood or urine specimens to sustain the illusion of illness. Most often, sufferers from factitious disorder do what they do based on a warped need for attention from others and the desire for an abnormally intense and dependent relationship with the child.

been, who a person is, or even entire conversations. Often this is prompted by a stressful event, such as abuse, a traumatic experience similar to those detailed in the section on PTSD, or the death of a loved one. Memory loss is the primary symptom of this disorder, which is more common among young adults.

DISSOCIATIVE FUGUE. Dissociative fugue (pronounced fyoog) is a particularly disturbing mental phenomenon as it involves one or more instances of a person leaving their normal, everyday life for a period of time and taking up a new life, with no recollection of their former life. Like dissociative amnesia, fugues are often triggered by traumatic events and are often fueled by unfulfilled wishes. An individual in the midst of a fugue will often leave home, abandoning all aspects of his or her life, and assume a new identity in another place. A fugue can last hours or days or longer.

DISSOCIATIVE IDENTITY DISORDER. Dissociative identity disorder, or DID (formerly known as multiple personality disorder, or MPD), involves an individual having two or more identities or personalities that are in control of an individual's behaviors and thoughts at different times. A controversial diagnosis (as it violates the basic belief that only one person can inhabit a body), people diagnosed with DID will often have a variety of personalities that are very different from one another and that may be in opposition to one another. For example, one personality may require an individual to wear glasses in order to see clearly, while another personality will not wear glasses. Or one personality may be left-handed whereas the other(s) are right-handed. DID usually begins in childhood and is often the result of severe trauma or an individual's repressing, or keeping back, strong feelings and desires.

Because of the association of the concept of repression (holding back painful memories) with dissociative disorders, psychoanalytic therapists seem to have good success in treating these disorders (for an explanation of the principles of psychoanalysis, see Chapter 15: Mental Health Therapies). Hypnosis may be also be used by psychoanalysts to help uncover forgotten memories in order to get to the root of why individuals disconnect from themselves.

Personality Disorders

People have different personalities (one's behavioral and emotional traits). Many people, however, share a type of personality, which means they have certain tendencies. For example, an individual who is sensitive to criticism might have an avoidant personality type. This is perfectly acceptable unless that person's behavior is extreme, thereby presenting problems in personal relationships and the ability to function in society. If one avoids people in social and work-related situations out of fear of being criticized or rejected; shies away from getting close to other people for fear of being made fun of; has low self-esteem; and is painfully shy and standoffish, that person might have an avoidant personality disorder. In other words, the difference between a personality type and a personality disorder is that the disorder separates people from others and the separation can prevent them from being happy and successful.

There is a wide range of personality disorders. There is the histrionic personality disorder, in which an individual needs to be the center of attention; behaves inappropriately (making sexual comments, for example); wears revealing clothes; is overly dramatic; is easily influenced by other people or events; and exaggerates how emotionally close one actually is to another person.

Dependent personality disorder is marked by an overwhelming need for advice and reassurance from others; being unable to disagree with others for fear he or she will no longer be liked; having a lack of initiative and self-direction; and showing an unusual need for close relationships along with a fear of being alone.

Other personality disorders include the paranoid personality disorder (which involves constant distrust and suspicion of other people; thinks oth-

MENTAL ILLNESS IN THE MOVIES

Over the years, a great number of films have presented audiences with characters struggling with a mental illness. Sometimes, filmmakers are able to humanize the face of mental illness and demystify it by showing everyday people triumphing over a disorder. Other times, filmmakers have reached into the darkest depths of the human psyche and created terrifying characters with mental problems so severe that the individuals are a threat to others and themselves. The following films include characters with varying degrees and types of mental illness:

Benny and Joon

Cape Fear

Desperately Seeking Susan

Fatal Attraction

Girl Interrupted

Good Will Hunting

Hamlet

High Anxiety

I Never Promised You a Rose Garden

One Flew over the Cuckoo's Nest

Ordinary People

Primal Fear

Psycho

Rainman

Silence of the Lambs

Spellbound

Splendor in the Grass

Sybil

The Glass Menagerie

The Other Sister

The Prince of Tides

The Three Faces of Eve

Vertigo

What's Eating Gilbert Grape?

ers are "out to get them."). There is also the schizoid personality disorder (in which people are removed from social contact with others and have problems experiencing and expressing emotion). Another is the borderline personality disorder (wherein an individual is unstable in relationships with others, has poor self-image and extremist thinking, and is very impulsive). Lastly, there is the narcissistic personality disorder (wherein an individual is overly conceited, having an abnormal need for admiration and lack of empathy for others).

Personality disorders are treated differently, depending upon which type of disorder is present. The difficulty lies in the fact that personality disorders carry risks with them that can affect treatment and a person's personal safety. For instance, people with severe personality disorders often engage in high-risk behavior, such as excessive drinking or taking illegal drugs. Furthermore, they are particularly vulnerable to psychiatric breakdowns, are less likely to take medications prescribed to them in the proper manner, and have a hard time taking responsibility for their behavior or trusting their mental health care provider.

FOR MORE INFORMATION

Books

Cush, Cathie. *Depression (Teen Hot Line)*. Raintree/Steck Vaughn, 1994.

Friedland, Bruce. *Personality Disorders (Psychological Disorders and Their Treatment)*. Chelsea House, 1991.

Ingersoll, Barbara D. *Distant Drums, Different Drummers: A Guide for Young People with ADHD*. Cape Publications, 1995.

Klebanoff, Susan and Ellen Luborsky. *Ups and Downs: How to Beat the Blues and Teen Depression*. New York: Price Stern Sloan, Inc. 1999.

Levine, Mel, Melvin D. Levine, and Ann Jennings. *Keeping a Head in School: A Student's Book About Learning Abilities and Learning Disorders*. Educator's Publishing Service, Inc., 1991.

Roleff, Tamara L., ed. *Suicide: Opposing Viewpoints*. Greenhaven Press, 1997.

Sebastian, Richard. Solomon H. Snyder and Dale C. Garell, eds. *Compulsive Behavior (Encyclopedia of Health Series: Psychological Disorders and Their Treatment)*. Chelsea House, 1993.

Web sites

American Psychiatric Association. [Online] http://www.psych.org (Accessed July 28, 1999).

mental illness

American Psychological Association. [Online] http://www.apa.org/ (Accessed July 28, 1999).

OC Foundation of California. [Online] http://www.ocdhelp.org/faq.html (Accessed July 28, 1999).

Yellow Ribbon Suicide Prevention Program. [Online] http://www.yellowribbon.org (Accessed July 28, 1999).

13

Eating Disorders

Eating disorders are dangerous psychological (relating to the mind) illnesses that affect millions of people, especially young women and girls. The most widely known eating disorders are anorexia nervosa and bulimia nervosa, which will be discussed further in this chapter.

Officially recognized by the medical community only since 1980, eating disorders were first brought to the public's attention when pop singer Karen Carpenter (1953–83) died from complications resulting from anorexia. People suffering from eating disorders battle life-threatening obsessions with food and unhealthy thoughts about their body weight and shape. If untreated, these disorders can lead to death. Researchers have found many factors that are probable causes of eating disorders. Recovery from an eating disorder is possible, though it is a difficult process that should not be done alone. The first steps toward recovery are for the sufferer to accept that there is a problem and to show a willingness to focus on his or her feelings rather than on food and weight.

This chapter will discuss the types of eating disorders that have been identified, the causes, the consequences of an eating disorder on the mind and body, and the treatment and prevention of eating disorders.

TYPES OF EATING DISORDERS AND THEIR CHARACTERISTICS

Anorexia Nervosa

Anorexia nervosa is a condition in which a person refuses to maintain a healthy body weight (persons whose weight is at least 15 percent below their normal body weight might fall into this category). The term anorexia nervosa means literally "nervous lack of appetite." However, this name is misleading as people with anorexia do not lack an appetite; rather, they battle hunger every day. Anorectics, as people who suffer from anorexia are referred to, are extremely afraid of gaining weight or becoming what they perceive to be fat.

Typically, what accompanies this fear of becoming fat is an anorectic's faulty perception of her body. Some anorectics may realize that they are indeed thin but will still view a particular part of their bodies, such as the stomach or thighs, as being fat and out of proportion. In fact, an anorectic's self-esteem is closely tied to this distorted view of her body. Continued weight loss is considered by anorectics to be a sign of achievement and self-discipline while any weight gain, even if it brings them closer to a healthy body weight, is considered a sign of weakness or a lack of self-control.

Anorexia is often difficult to diagnose and treat because of the secretive nature of this illness. Anorectics are usually good at concealing their self-starvation with excuses, or they may even engage in purging (vomiting) if forced to eat. Furthermore, anorectics will often wear heavy clothes that both

WORDS TO KNOW

Adrenaline: A hormone that is released during times of stress and fear.

Amenorrhea: The absence of menstrual cycles.

Anorexia nervosa: A term meaning "lack of appetite"; an eating disorder marked by a person's refusal to maintain a healthy body weight through restricting food intake or other means.

Binge-eating disorder: An eating disorder that involves repetitive episodes of binge eating in a restricted period of time over several months.

Bingeing: When an individual eats, in a particular period of time, an abnormally large amount of food.

Body set-point theory: Theory of weight control that claims that the body will defend a certain weight regardless of factors such as calorie intake and exercise.

Bulimia nervosa: A term that means literally "ox hunger"; an eating disorder characterized by a repeated cycle of bingeing and purging.

Depression: Common psychological problem characterized by intense and prolonged feelings of sadness and hopelessness.

Diuretic: A drug that expels water from the body through urination.

Edema: Swelling.

Endorphin: Any of a group of natural proteins in the brain known as natural painkillers that make people feel good after exercising.

Enema: A process that expels waste from the body by injecting liquid into the anus.

Epidemiology: The study of disease in a population.

Exercise addiction: Also known as compulsive exercise, a condition in which participation in exercise activities is taken to an extreme; an individual exercises to the detriment of all other things in his or her life.

Hypertension: High blood pressure.

Lanugo: Fine hair that grows all over the body to keep it warm when the body lacks enough fat to accomplish this.

Laxative: A drug that induces bowel movements.

Obesity: The condition of being very overweight.

Purging: When a person gets rid of the food that she has eaten by vomiting, taking an excessive amount of laxatives, diuretics, or enemas or engaging in fasting and/or excessive exercise.

Russell's sign: Calluses, cuts, and sores on the knuckles from repeated self-induced vomiting.

camouflage (hide) their excessive weight loss from others and keep them warm. (Due to their dangerously low weight and lack of insulating body fat, anorectics are often cold.)

In addition to avoiding eating whenever possible, anorectics will often display high levels of energy that seem at odds with their frail physical conditions. Anorectics may also develop odd oral habits, including chewing gum throughout the day, drinking an excessive amount of coffee or diet soda, and chain-smoking. Finally, many anorectics become obsessed with food, despite their unwillingness to consume any.

Bulimia Nervosa

Bulimia nervosa means literally "ox hunger." This term is appropriate on many levels as bulimia is characterized by a repeated cycle of binge eating and purging. A binge is when an individual eats, in a particular period of time, an abnormally large amount of food. (Of course, this doesn't refer to special occasions, such as holiday meals, when it is acceptable to eat more than usual.)

The binge is then followed by an episode of purging. Purging is when a person gets rid of the food that she has eaten by either making herself vomit, taking an excessive amount of laxatives (drugs that induce bowel movements), diuretics (drugs that expel water from the body through urination), or enemas (a process that expels waste from the body by injecting liquid into the anus), or engaging in fasting and/or excessive exercise. People with bulimia, known as bulimics, engage in such behaviors at least two times a week for a period of six months or more.

A particularly stressful event or depression often triggers an episode of binge eating, intense hunger that follows restricted food intake, or a variety of feelings tied to body weight, body image, and food. The binge eating may temporarily relieve a bulimic's feelings of depression or stress, but often deeper feelings of depression, disappointment, and anxiety may follow. This will then trigger an episode of purging. Many bulimics report feeling out of control when bingeing and use similar terms to describe their need to purge their bodies of the food they just consumed.

Bulimics, like anorectics, are usually ashamed of their behavior and will attempt to

Pop singer Karen Carpenter, who died from complications as a result of anorexia at the age of 30. (AP/Wide World Photos. Reproduced by permission.)

Eating disorders are often difficult to diagnose and treat because of the secretive nature of these illnesses. (Photograph © 1995 Science Photo Library/Custom Medical Stock Photo. Reproduced by permission.)

EATING DISORDERS NAMED

English physician Richard Morton first documented cases of self-starvation in the seventeenth century. The term anorexia nervosa was later coined by French neurologist Charles Lasegue and English physician Sir William Gull in the mid-1870s. The symptoms of bulimia (bingeing and purging) were not recognized as a separate condition from self-starvation until the 1940s. English physician Gerald Russell formally named bulimia nervosa in 1979.

hide their illness from others. Because of this and the fact that many bulimics maintain a normal body weight, it is often hard to recognize that a person is, in fact, bulimic.

Many bulimics suffer from low self-esteem and may even have suicidal thoughts. Often they are rigid perfectionists who think in absolutes ("I am bad because I ate that"). Like anorectics, bulimics will make negative statements about their appearance and experience extreme guilt over eating even normal portions of food. They will begin to withdraw from social activities, particularly those that will make it difficult for them to purge without suspicion.

Other Types of Disordered Eating

There are those individuals whose behavior does not fall under the categories of anorexia or bulimia; rather, these people can exhibit a wide range of disordered eating and unhealthy weight management symptoms. Since they cannot be diagnosed as anorexic or bulimic, these individuals will typically receive a diagnosis of an "eating disorder not otherwise specified." An example of disordered eating includes a person of normal weight who eats no fat and occasionally purges. She would not be considered bulimic because she is not bingeing, and she also is not anorectic because she is not dangerously underweight. She would therefore be diagnosed with an eating disorder not otherwise specified.

There are other disorders, such as binge-eating disorder and exercise addiction, that are not yet official psychological diagnoses but which are becoming more and more prevalent. These problems are often diagnosed as "eating disorder not otherwise specified" as well. They often occur in conjunction with anorexia and bulimia. However, they can also occur independently of other disordered eating and may soon have their own official diagnoses.

BINGE-EATING DISORDER. Like bulimia, binge-eating disorder involves repetitive episodes of binge eating in a restricted period of time over several months. This illness is different from bulimia, however, because people suffering from binge-eating disorder do not purge after a binge. This disorder has more to do with an absolute lack of control over eating than with the conciliatory acts (purging) that follow a bulimic's binge.

Binge eaters will eat very rapidly, usually until they are uncomfortably full. They will eat big portions of food even if they are not actually hungry. Because of this, many binge eaters engage in binges secretively as they are embarrassed by how much they have eaten and feel guilty and depressed following these episodes. Similar to the binges experienced by bulimics, binge eaters report that depression and anxiety usually trigger their binges. During the binge itself, sufferers often feel out of control or disconnected from their actions.

Binge eaters usually suffer from obesity (being very overweight). Furthermore, many have been "yo-yo" dieters (experiencing large fluctuations in weight from a cycle of dieting) their entire lives. Both of these effects can cause binge eaters to feel worse about their inability to control their eating habits. (Not everyone who is obese suffers from binge-eating disorder. Rather, obesity must be paired with certain behaviors for it to be evidence of binge-eating disorder.)

EATING DISORDER STATISTICS

Eating disorder organizations qualify that eating disorder statistics are estimates because the illnesses are often hidden and difficult to diagnose. It is likely that the actual figures are higher than they appear due to the secretive nature of eating disorders.

- About 8 million people in the United States suffer from an eating disorder. Among young women, it is estimated that 15 percent suffer from some kind of disordered eating behavior.

- Females make up 90 to 95 percent of the people who suffer from anorexia.

- 1 percent of young women between the ages of ten and twenty have anorexia.

- 85 percent of the time, anorexia starts between the ages of thirteen and twenty.

- 10 to 15 percent of anorectics will die from the disease.

- 2 to 5 percent of anorectics will commit suicide.

- About 1,000 women die from anorexia each year.

- 30 to 50 percent of anorectics in treatment show signs of bulimia as well.

- 4 percent of college-aged women have bulimia.

- 10 to 15 percent of people with bulimia are male.

- Of psychological disorders, eating disorders have the highest rate of deaths.

- About 60 percent of eating disorder sufferers recover with treatment.

These statistics are based on information from the following organizations: Anorexia Nervosa and Related Eating Disorders, Inc.; American Anorexia/Bulimia Association, Inc.; and National Depressive and Manic-Depressive Association.

Christy Henrich, a competitive gymnast, died in 1994 after a long battle with two eating disorders that had reduced her weight to just 60 pounds. (AP/Wide World Photos. Reproduced by permission.)

Other signs of binge-eating disorder can include food disappearing from cabinets and cupboards at a rapid rate, or even finding an excessive amount of food wrappers concealed under someone's bed or in her trash. The consumption of odd foodstuffs such as raw cookie dough or condiments can also point to binge-eating disorder.

EXERCISE ADDICTION. Exercise addiction, or compulsive exercise, seems like a strange term as most people consider exercise to be good for their health. Exercise is a fun way to relieve stress and increase energy levels. It releases endorphins (the body's natural painkillers, which make people feel good after exercising). However, when a person's interest and participation in exercise activities are taken to extremes, exercise can turn into an addiction that must be performed each day; the act of exercising provides that person with a temporary high. If an exercise-addicted person cannot exercise, he or she will experience a great deal of guilt and anxiety over the inactivity.

Exercise-addicted individuals will exercise to the detriment of everything else in their lives. Someone who is addicted to exercise will exercise with serious physical injuries, pass up opportunities to spend time with loved ones in favor of exercise, and even miss work or school to spend time exercising. Depression, low self-esteem, and repressed anger are all characteristics of exercise-addicted individuals because no matter how much they exercise or achieve in other areas of their lives, they believe they should do more.

Because some sports demand a certain body type (such as gymnastics or ice skating) or depend on how much a person weighs (such as wrestling or horse racing), exercise addiction often develops in elite athletes like dancers, ice skaters, gymnasts, jockeys, and wrestlers, in their quest to perform the best in their sport. Exercise addiction can also be linked to those suffering from anorexia or bulimia because they feel unsatisfied with their bodies and think excessive exercise can help them get thin. Bulimics will often use compulsive exercise as a method of purging.

CAUSES OF EATING DISORDERS

A number of factors contribute to the development of eating disorders. Some are biological and genetic in nature, while others are a direct result of the cultural and familial environment in which an individual is raised.

MALES WITH EATING DISORDERS

Although eating disorders affect women more than men, a large number of males suffer from anorexia nervosa and bulimia nervosa as well as binge-eating disorder and exercise addiction. In fact, 5 to 10 percent of people suffering from anorexia are male, and approximately 10 to 15 percent of people with bulimia are male. The percentages may even be higher as some experts suspect that few men actually seek help because they are ashamed and embarrassed that they have what has come to be viewed as a "female" problem.

Many male eating-disorder sufferers participate or have participated in a sport that demands a certain body type, such as wrestling and running. Wrestlers are a notoriously high-risk group because many try to lose additional pounds rapidly just prior to a match. This allows the wrestler to compete in a lower weight-class while having developed the skill and strength for a higher weight-class in practice. To accomplish this rapid weight loss, unhealthy weight reduction methods, such as fasting and purging, are often used.

Being overweight in childhood can also influence the development of an eating disorder in males. And dieting, a well-known trigger for eating disorders, can start the development of disordered eating in males.

Biological Factors

There are factors contributing to the development of eating disorders that are biological, or genetic. For example, if a person has a relative in her immediate family with an eating disorder, she is at a higher risk to develop an eating disorder.

Additional biological factors contributing to disordered eating can be triggered by the initial act of starving, binge-eating, or purging. This is because these behaviors can change an individual's chemical balance, particularly brain chemistry. Starvation and overeating lead to the production of brain chemicals that induce feelings of peace and euphoria (happiness). These good feelings mask feelings of anxiety and depression, both of which are commonly experienced by people suffering from eating disorders. This has caused certain researchers to conclude that some people with eating disorders use (or do not use) food as a relief when they are feeling poorly about themselves.

Of note is the fact that certain researchers believe that depression, which is also genetic, can be the cause of an eating disorder. (See section on depression later in this chapter.)

Psychological Factors

People suffering from eating disorders share many of the same personality traits. For example, eating-disordered people lean toward being perfectionists. Furthermore, many of them suffer from feelings of low self-esteem, despite their accomplishments and perfectionist ways. Extremist thinking, too, is present in many people with eating disorders. These individuals assume that if being thin is "good" then being even thinner is better. This leads to the thought that being the thinnest is the absolute best; it is this thinking that pushes some anorectics to plummet to body weights of fifty or sixty pounds.

Often, people who live with eating disorders have no sense of self. They simply do not feel that they know who they are or what their place in the world is. An eating disorder, however, offers a sense of identity to these individuals in that it enables them to say, "I am thin," and "I am dieting." This eventually leads them to define themselves solely on their appearance and their dangerous actions rather than with positive, healthy accomplishments.

Social Factors

Eating disorders, in general, occur primarily in industrialized societies, such as the United States, Australia, Canada, Europe, and Japan. In all of these places, the media (TV, movies, magazines) bombard people with the virtues and importance of being thin. It is endlessly implied in television

Many people with eating disorders have a distorted view of their bodies, seeing themselves as overweight when, in fact, they are not. (Photograph by Robert J. Huffman. Field Mark Publications. Reproduced by permission.)

shows, movies, and advertisements that thinness will bring a person success, power, approval, popularity, friends, and romantic relationships. Women, in particular, are held to an almost-impossible-to-achieve standard of physical fitness and beauty, the height of which is being slender and thin. (In fact, female fashion models now weigh an average of 25 percent less than an av-

To match the proportions of a Barbie doll, a woman with a normal shape (left) would have to transform her height, waist, and bust to appear like the figure on the right. (Photograph by Jill Greenberg © 1996. Reprinted with permission of Discover Magazine.)

erage woman.) Because of these media messages, and correlating comments from young women about their weight and body shape, a link between eating disorders and social pressures can be established.

Family Factors

People are shaped in part by their experiences with their families. Families contribute to an individual's emotional growth. If someone is raised in a dysfunctional family, she may have feelings of abandonment and loneliness. Certain families have dynamics in which rigidity, overprotectiveness, and emotional distance are commonplace. If parents make all of a child's decisions for her, when she gets to adolescence and needs to make decisions for herself, she may find she doesn't have the tools to do so. All of these dynamics can promote the development of eating disorders in the future.

Families in which unrealistically high expectations are placed on the children can also lead these individuals to develop disordered eating. The disordered eating is used as a way to cope with feelings of inadequacy and as a way to control at least one area of their lives.

Children also receive their first messages about their bodies from their families. If parents place too much emphasis on physical appearance, it can lead to low self-esteem in those children, placing them at risk for developing eating disorders when they are older.

Most children learn their eating habits and food preferences from their families. Often times, cleaning one's plate or not eating too much or even parents' close control of what their child eats can lead to disordered eating later in life. Parents' attitudes toward food and their own bodies greatly affect children's attitudes toward food and how they will feel about themselves.

Triggers

Triggers are items or events that spark the beginning of other events. Eating disorders are often triggered by an event or a circumstance in the life of an individual who is already prone to developing such a condition. A period of adjustment, such as leaving home to attend summer camp, prep school,

Actress Ally Sheedy. (AP/Wide World Photos. Reproduced by permission.)

FAMOUS PEOPLE WHO HAVE BATTLED EATING DISORDERS

Paula Abdul, Singer

Justine Bateman, Actor

Karen Carpenter, Singer*

Nadia Comaneci, Gymnast

Susan Dey, Actor

Diana, Princess of Wales

Jane Fonda, Actor/Activist

Zina Garrison, Tennis Player

Tracy Gold, Actor

Heidi Guenther, Ballet Dancer*

Margaux Hemingway, Actor

Christy Henrich, Gymnast*

Daniel Johns, Musician

Kathy Johnson, Gymnast

Gelsey Kirkland, Ballet Dancer

Lucy Lawless, Actor

Gilda Radner, Actor/Comic

Cathy Rigby, Gymnast

Joan Rivers, Comic

Ally Sheedy, Actor

* indicates death resulting from the eating disorder

or college, can easily trigger disordered eating in an individual with such tendencies already in place. A traumatic event in someone's life, such as sexual abuse, can also trigger the development of an eating disorder. Other triggers can seem harmless yet represent large life changes, such as moving, starting a new school or job, graduation, and even marriage. Whatever the trigger is, it is usually closely tied to the end of a valued relationship or a feeling of loneliness.

The most common trigger of an eating disorder, however, is dieting. Very often dieting can lead people to disordered eating of some sort, including anorexia or bulimia.

THE PHYSICAL AND PSYCHOLOGICAL CONSEQUENCES OF EATING DISORDERS

An eating disorder can have serious physical and psychological consequences. How serious these consequences are depends on how early an eating disorder is identified and treated. With help, the effects of an eating disorder can be treated; however, if an eating disorder is left untreated for years, some of the effects are irreversible and life-threatening. For these reasons, early detection and treatment is essential and can save a person's life.

The different types of eating disorders are often connected. In fact, 30 to 50 percent of people with anorexia exhibit signs of bulimia as well. Therefore, the consequences of the disorders are also connected. In other words, bulimia and anorexia often share physical, as well as psychological, consequences.

How Anorexia Nervosa Affects the Body

Anorexia causes many physical problems. For instance, it upsets the normal functions of hormones. For girls, this means the body is unable to produce enough of the female hormone estrogen because it does not have enough fat. This will cause an absence of menstrual cycles, called amenorrhea. For boys, anorexia causes a decrease in the production of the male hormone testosterone, which results in a loss of sexual interest.

An anorectic body lacks the protective layer of fat it needs to stay warm. To compensate for the lack of fat, lanugo (fine hair) will grow all over the body to keep it warm. Another problem anorexia causes is a decrease in bone mass. The body needs calcium for strong bones. Since an anorectic is not eating enough food, which is the source of calcium, the body's bones suffer and weaken. Later in life, this could result in a dangerous bone disease called osteoporosis.

Additionally, without the fuel it needs, an anorectic's body will respond as if it is being assaulted and begins to fight back in order to survive. To survive the body must have energy, but because the body has no food to turn into energy, it seeks out the muscles, and eventually, the organs (heart, kidney, and brain) for sustenance—often causing permanent damage to the organs in the process. This is the most serious consequence of anorexia and can possibly lead to cardiac arrest and/or kidney failure, both of which can result in death.

How Bulimia Nervosa Affects the Body

The frequent purging that occurs with bulimia does serious damage to the body. Self-induced vomiting can severely damage the digestive system. Repeated vomiting also damages the esophagus (throat) and eventually it may tear and bleed. Vomiting brings stomach acids into the mouth, causing the enamel on the teeth to wear away. As a result, the teeth may become weakened and appear ragged. There will also be an increase in cavities from vomiting.

Other consequences include swollen salivary glands, which gives some bulimics the appearance of having chipmunk cheeks, and cuts and sores on the knuckles from repeatedly sticking one's fingers down the throat to induce vomiting (known as "Russell's sign"). Stomach cramps and difficulty in swallowing are also common.

If laxatives (drugs that induce bowel movements) are abused, constipation will result because the body can no longer produce a bowel movement on its own. Abuse of laxatives and diuretics (drugs that expel water from the body through urination) can also cause bloating, water retention, and edema (swelling) of the stomach. Because the body is constantly being denied the nutrients and fluids it needs to survive, the kidneys and heart will also suffer. Specifically, a lack of potassium will result in cardiac abnormalities and possible kidney failure, which can also result in death.

How Binge-Eating Disorder Affects the Body

The physical effects of binge eating are not as severe as with anorexia and bulimia, namely because the body is not denied food or put through the painful process of purging. Nevertheless, there are some potentially serious consequences for binge eaters.

Since binge eaters may suffer from obesity, health complications such as diabetes or heart problems can develop. Health problems from yo-yo dieting can include hypertension (high blood pressure) and long-term damage to major organs, such as the kidney, liver, heart, and other muscles.

How Exercise Addiction Affects the Body

Many anorectics and bulimics exercise compulsively (constantly) in order to lose weight. Compulsive exercise is extremely dangerous and can cause many painful injuries, including stress fractures, damaged bones and joints, as well as torn muscles, ligaments, and tendons. Even worse, the injuries may become more serious as many compulsive exercisers will continue their routines despite their injuries.

When an eating disorder is successfully treated, the body can heal and return to normal. Sometimes, however, the eating disorder has continued for so many years that there is too much damage for a full recovery to occur. A person may have to live with a weak heart or kidney for the rest of her life. A woman may be unable to conceive a child because her reproductive system cannot function properly (due to the absence of menstruation). Also, a person may have to live with the debilitating bone disease osteoporosis.

How Eating Disorders Affect the Mind

The psychological consequences of an eating disorder are complex and difficult to overcome. An eating disorder is often a symptom of a larger problem in a person's life. The disorder is an unhealthy way for that person to

While exercise is good for most people, exercise addiction can lead to serious physical injuries, and more, if not controlled. (Photo Researchers, Inc. Reproduced by permission.)

cope with the painful emotions tied to the problem. For this reason, the emotional problems that triggered the eating disorder in the first place can worsen as the disorder takes hold.

An eating disorder can also cause more problems to surface in a person's life. Eating disorders make it difficult for people to perceive things normally because certain chemical changes take place when the body is deprived of nutrients. As a result, the body relies on adrenaline (a hormone that is normally released during times of stress and fear) instead of food for energy. Adrenaline naturally makes makes someone excited, which makes it more difficult to deal with painful emotions.

Research has shown that many people suffering from an eating disorder also suffer from other psychological problems. Sometimes the eating disorder causes other problems, and sometimes the problems coexist with the eating disorder. Some of the psychological disorders that can accompany an eating disorder include depression, obsessive-compulsive disorder, and anxiety and panic disorders.

In addition to having other psychological disorders, a person with an eating disorder may also engage in destructive behaviors as a result of low self-esteem. Just as an eating disorder is a negative way to cope with emotional problems, other destructive behaviors, such as self-mutilation, drug addiction, and alcoholism, are similar negative coping mechanisms.

Not everyone who has an eating disorder suffers from additional psychological disorders; however, it is very common. For this reason, psychological counseling is an essential part of recovery (see Chapter 15: Mental Health Therapies).

DEPRESSION. Depression is one of the most common psychological problems related to an eating disorder. It is characterized by intense and prolonged feelings of sadness and hopelessness. In its most serious form, depression may lead to suicide (the taking of one's own life). Considering that an eating disorder is often kept a secret, a person who is suffering feels alienated and alone. A person may feel that it is impossible to openly express her feelings. As a result, feelings of depression will worsen the effects of an eating disorder, making it difficult to break the cycle of disordered eating.

Feelings of depression will worsen the effects of an eating disorder, making it difficult to break the cycle of disordered eating. (Photograph by Robert J. Huffman. Field Mark Publications. Reproduced by permission.)

With counseling and support, it is possible to combat these negative feelings and prevent them from progressing over time. Recently, doctors have begun to prescribe antidepressant drugs, such as Prozac, to address the problems of depression resulting from an eating disorder. Prozac can help ease feelings of depression, which in turn gives a person better tools with which to fight an eating disorder. [For more information on depression, see Chapter 12: Mental Illness.]

OBSESSIVE-COMPULSIVE BEHAVIOR. Obsessions are constant thoughts that produce anxiety and stress. Compulsions are irrational behaviors that are repeated to reduce anxiety and stress. People with eating disorders are constantly thinking about food, calories, eating, and weight. As a result, they show signs of obsessive-compulsive behavior. If people with eating disorders also show signs of obsessive-compulsive behavior with things not related to food, they may be diagnosed with Obsessive-Compulsive Disorder (OCD).

Some obsessive-compulsive behaviors practiced by eating disorder sufferers include storing large amounts of food, collecting recipes, weighing themselves several times a day, and thinking constantly about the food they feel they should not eat. These obsessive thoughts and rituals worsen when the body is regularly deprived of food. Being in a state of starvation causes people to become so preoccupied with everything they have denied themselves that they think of little else.

FEELINGS OF ANXIETY, GUILT, AND SHAME. Everyone experiences feelings of anxiety (fear and worry), guilt, and shame at some time; however, these feelings become more intense with the onset of an eating disorder. Eating disorder sufferers fear that others will discover their illness. There is also a tremendous fear of gaining weight.

As the eating disorder progresses, body image becomes more distorted and the eating disorder becomes all-consuming. Some sufferers are often terrified of letting go of the illness, which causes many to protect their secret eating disorder even more.

Eating disorder sufferers have a strong need to control their environment and will avoid social situations where they may have to be around food in front of other people or where they may have to change their behavior. The anxiety that results causes people with eating disorders to be inflexible and rigid with their emotions.

Bulimics and binge eaters, specifically, experience guilt and shame with their disorders. This

SYMPTOMS OF DEPRESSION

- Extreme mood swings
- Inability to experience pleasure in anything
- Feelings of worthlessness
- Withdrawal from family and friends
- Constant fatigue (exhaustion)
- Insomnia (sleeplessness) or sleeping too much
- Loss of appetite or compulsive eating
- Inability to concentrate or make decisions
- Poor memory
- Unexplained headaches, backaches, or stomachaches

is mainly because, unlike anorectics, they are not usually in denial and they do realize that there is a problem. Bulimics will feel anxiety before, during, and after a binge and can only relieve this anxiety through purging. Purging, however, brings on overwhelming feelings of guilt and shame.

Binge eaters also feel anxiety during a binge, but because they do not purge, they feel ashamed over their lack of control around food.

EATING DISORDERS AND OTHER DESTRUCTIVE BEHAVIORS

Drug Addiction and Alcoholism

It is common for people with eating disorders also to struggle with drug and alcohol addiction. In fact, research shows that one-third of bulimics have a substance-abuse problem, particularly with stimulants (drugs that excite the nervous system) and alcohol. This may stem from the fact that people with eating disorders have difficulty coping with their emotions and use negative means, such as drugs, to mask their problems. Drugs and alcohol provide temporary escapes from reality but, similar to eating disorders, can progress into serious problems that require treatment to overcome. [For more information on drug addiction and alcoholism, see Chapter 14: Habits and Behaviors.]

Self-Mutilation

Self-mutilation is practiced by many eating disorder sufferers. It is also known as self-inflicted violence (SIV) or "cutting." The most common forms of self-mutilation include cutting, burning, head-banging, hitting, and biting oneself. The reasons people self-mutilate stem from an inability to handle overwhelming feelings or a state of emotional numbness. Many sufferers explain that they hurt themselves in order to distract themselves from emotional pain because it is easier to deal with physical pain than to address uncomfortable emotions, such as fear or anger. They may also hurt themselves in order to feel something which gives them an escape from feelings of loneliness. [For more information on self-mutilation, see Chapter 14: Habits and Behaviors.]

EATING DISORDERS AND SEXUALITY

Eating disorders often develop around puberty, when the body is changing and maturing. This time of change can produce anxiety and confusion for both boys and girls because puberty is the beginning of sexual maturity. Girls develop breasts, start menstruating, grow taller, and develop more body hair. Boys' sexual organs (the penis and testicles) grow. Boys also grow taller, get more body and facial hair, and develop bigger muscles.

The sexual feelings that accompany puberty are new, and what they are feeling or experiencing may embarrass some young people. When someone is suffering from an eating disorder, issues surrounding sexuality can become even more complicated. Some people may seek out sexual relationships to feel close to someone and ease feelings of isolation. Others may avoid sexual relationships altogether because they feel ashamed of their bodies.

In some cases, an eating disorder is triggered by sexual abuse (when a person is forced to engage in sexual activities against his or her will). In these instances, an eating disorder sufferer is usually acting out in response to a painful event. She may gain or lose weight in an attempt to make herself sexually undesirable. She may avoid sexual relations as a way to take control over her body and prevent painful feelings from resurfacing. The anger and distrust felt toward the opposite sex may result in complete rejection of the opposite sex. On the other hand, some eating disorder sufferers may have many sexual partners in an attempt to erase the past and gain acceptance from the opposite sex.

TREATMENT AND RECOVERY FROM EATING DISORDERS

Treatment and recovery go hand in hand. It is very hard to stop an eating disorder without any treatment. Recovery is a long process in which an eating disorder sufferer may have to enter treatment more than once. Some people may even try different kinds of treatment programs during their recovery until they find one that works for them.

There may be obstacles to starting treatment. The fear of becoming fat and losing control, which drives most eating disorders, is very strong and hard to eliminate. Also, an eating disorder sufferer may be in denial about her condition and may be unwilling to consider treatment. These feelings may be based on a fear of letting go of the illness that she feels is part of her identity. The eating disorder sufferer must learn to refocus her thoughts from food and weight to her emotions so that she can deal with what is really bothering her. Since many feelings that need to be addressed have been buried by the disorder, professional counseling is important for a successful recovery.

In order for treatment to work, a person must be ready to be treated. Some sufferers may even say they are ready but really are not. They may pretend to change their attitude about food, but they are still starving themselves or bingeing and purging their food secretively. If a person does not fully commit to a treatment program, she will most likely continue suffering from the deadly illness even after completion of the program.

Treatment Basics

Treatment programs vary in the approach that they take. An eating disorder sufferer needs to find a program that best suits her and her condition. A program may work for one person but be ineffective for another. It is important that the person feels comfortable with and believes in the treatment.

Treatment usually begins with an assessment by a physician or mental health counselor. Depending on the severity of the eating disorder, the sufferer will either enter an inpatient or outpatient program. Inpatient programs, or hospitalization, are for the most severe cases. To be hospitalized, the sufferer is usually at a critical point in her illness where her life is in danger or she may have strong suicidal thoughts. Outpatient programs are conducted at a facility or doctor's office that the patient visits while still living at home.

Whether the program is inpatient or outpatient, it will usually include various forms of counseling and medical care to treat the physical effects of the illness. The most common forms of counseling include nutrition, individual, family, and group. Nutrition counseling teaches the patient about healthy eating habits and designs appropriate meals. Its goal is to slowly bring the sufferer's weight back up to a safe level that can be easily maintained without dieting or provoking obsessive behavior about food. The first few months of treatment for anorectics can be very dangerous if the eating disorder has gone on for a long time. This is due to the shock the body experiences from eating food after years of starvation.

WORDS OF RECOVERY

Mostly what happened was that my life took over—that is to say, that the impulse for life became stronger in me than the impulse for death. In me, the two impulses coexist in an uneasy balance, but they are balanced enough now that I am alive.

Looking back, I see that what I did then was pretty basic. I took a leap of faith. And I believe that has made all the difference. I hung on to the only thing that seemed real to me, and that was a basic ethical principle; if I was alive, then I had a responsibility to stay alive and do something with the life I had been given. And though I was not at all convinced, when I made that leap of faith, that I had any sensible reason for doing so—

though I did not fully believe that there was anything that could possibly make as much sense as an eating disorder—I made it because I began to wonder. I simply began to wonder, in the same way I had wondered what would happen if I began to lose weight, what would happen if I stopped. It was worth it.

It is worth it. It's a fight. It's exhausting, but it is a fight I believe in. I cannot believe, anymore, in the fight between body and soul. If I do, it will kill me. But more importantly, if I do, I have taken the easy way out. I know for a fact that sickness is easier.

But health is more interesting.

Excerpted from Marya Hornbacher, *Wasted: A Memoir of Anorexia and Bulimia*. New York: HarperFlamingo, 1998, p. 280.

Individual counseling is one-on-one counseling in which a therapist helps the sufferer deal with her emotions and take control of her body and life again. Family counseling is when the family of the eating disorder sufferer is involved. This type of counseling helps the family and the sufferer to establish better relationships and change any unhealthy dynamics of the family. In group counseling, a counselor leads meetings of a group of eating disorder sufferers to help them learn how to achieve and maintain strong relationships. It also helps sufferers learn that they are not alone.

In support groups, eating disorder sufferers meet to offer support, understanding, and hope to one another as they battle their disorders. Support groups, like group counseling, help sufferers to not feel so alone in their illnesses and learn from others' experiences.

Some eating disorder sufferers will be prescribed medication to ease depression and anxiety as part of their treatment.

These people are attending a support group meeting of Overeaters Anonymous to help with their eating disorder. (Photograph © by Carolyn A. McKeone. Photo Researchers, Inc. Reproduced by permission.)

[For more information on types of treatments and therapy, see Chapter 15: Mental Health Therapies.]

The Recovery Process

Recovery is not easy. Most eating disorder sufferers feel that they are not worthy of love or life. It takes time (months, even years) and a lot of support from friends, family, and medical professionals to change the sufferers' self-perceptions. They need to feel worthy again of love from others. However, recovery is not as simple as saying "I love you" to eating disorder sufferers. They need to build their self-esteem so that they can believe that they deserve the love of others. Some people are able to make an initial recovery, but many find recovery to be an ongoing, lifelong process.

An eating disorder sufferer has certain goals, both physical and psychological, that she needs to try to reach in recovery. The physical aims should include the ability to eat a variety of healthful foods (without bingeing and purging) and maintain a healthy weight. Females should start their menstrual periods either for the first time or again without the help of medication.

The psychological aims of recovery should include a noticeable decrease in the fear of food and becoming fat as well as the ability to establish strong relationships with family and friends again. Another goal should be to realize the role society and the media play in furthering disordered thinking about people's weights and body shapes. This realization will help sufferers learn to accept and like their bodies without having to live up to unrealistic standards of beauty and thinness. An eating disorder sufferer should also work to establish new, positive coping skills and engage in activities that do not involve food or weight control.

The goals for recovery should start small. Learning to meet modest goals first will provide a sense of accomplishment that will help push a person toward meeting larger goals. It is easy to become overwhelmed and fall back into familiar patterns of living. Eating disorder sufferers have taught themselves how to starve or binge and purge and are familiar with using the disorder to help them cope with life. They need time to relearn healthy eating habits and how to feel good about themselves again at a healthy weight.

WHAT TO DO IF YOU THINK SOMEONE HAS AN EATING DISORDER

- First, voice concerns to the person privately.

- Listen carefully to what that person is saying.

- Avoid using judgmental statements.

- Let the person know that you are concerned about her health.

- Be familiar with some resources, such as reading materials, web sites, or community centers, that can be introduced to that person.

- If the person exhibits behaviors that are life-threatening, such as bingeing and purging several times a day, fainting, or expressing suicidal thoughts, tell a trusted adult immediately.

eating disorders

Many eating disorder organizations focus on prevention in their programs. That is, stopping eating disorders before they even start. The belief is that awareness and education can go a long way in preventing the onset of these painful illnesses, which can become lifelong struggles. Many eating disorder experts promote teaching prevention at a young age since eating disorders usually begin in adolescence, although there are reported cases of eating disorders starting in children as young as eight years old.

There are a few main objectives that eating disorder organizations focus on in their prevention programs. These objectives help to provide people with the tools they need to cope with the problems that may contribute to an eating disorder.

Prevention means:

- reordering thoughts on food and weight
- focusing on health
- understanding the dangers of dieting
- developing a positive body image
- rebelling against cultural and media messages that encourage unhealthy behaviors
- explaining why fat is not the enemy
- helping to end fat discrimination

Reordering Thoughts about Food and Weight

Since there is enormous pressure to be thin in many cultures, including the United States, many people are dissatisfied with how they look, believing that they are inadequate and unworthy of affection or love. As a result of a negative body image, many people go on strict diets and believe that food is the enemy. However, the body needs food to survive and going on restrictive diets will only lead to an intense preoccupation with food, calories, and weight.

The first step in preventing the development of eating disorders is to reorder feelings and thoughts about food and weight. Eating disorder experts recommend that people reject unhealthy messages about weight, body shape, and diet. Since body shape and weight are determined

Developing a positive body image is necessary to the prevention of eating disorders. Young people should not focus on what they weigh, but rather on maintaining a healthy lifestyle. (Photograph by Richard Hutchings. Photo Researchers, Inc. Reproduced by permission.)

mostly from genetics, there is only so much a person can do to control or change weight and body shape. Trying to fight against or change the body's set point (the weight at which one's body naturally falls) is unhealthy and possibly dangerous because it creates a cycle of yo-yo dieting. Research has shown that while not every diet leads to eating disorders, 80 percent of eating disorders are initially triggered by a diet. [See Chapter 1: Nutrition, for more information on body set point.]

DEVELOPING A POSITIVE BODY IMAGE

Developing a positive body image is necessary to the prevention of eating disorders. Many people struggle with this issue and must work hard at accepting their bodies. Eating disorder experts emphasize the importance of exercising for health reasons rather than for burning calories and losing weight. The same experts also recommend becoming politically active in the fight against unhealthy cultural messages because it can be a source of positive feelings and empowerment.

Other suggestions include:

- Avoid negative talk about food and weight.
- Avoid referring to foods as "good" or "bad."

HOW DOES DIETING AFFECT THE BODY AND MIND?

The body needs a certain amount of food to function properly. If caloric intake is restricted and the body falls below its set point, it will respond by lowering its metabolism. Metabolism is the rate at which the body burns energy. When the body doesn't get enough fuel to burn, it must learn to function on less. In response, the body will hold on to any food it gets and store fat more efficiently on fewer calories. Typically, when a person stops dieting, she will gain more weight than what was lost and be more likely to keep the extra weight because the body has made adjustments to compensate for a lack of food from the dieting.

The negative physical effects of dieting can include:

- headaches
- dizziness
- stomach pain
- iron deficiency that causes fatigue
- possible menstrual irregularity
- lack of estrogen
- calcium deficiency
- lack of growth from malnutrition

The negative psychological effects of dieting can include:

- preoccupation with food, eating, and calories
- increased irritability
- increased stress and anxiety from semi-starvation
- inability to determine hunger and fullness
- negative body image that can lead to depression and low self-esteem
- fear of food that can lead to isolation and alienation

- Don't participate in weight-loss programs or experiment with weight-loss products.
- Exercise moderately; don't engage in unhealthy or excessive exercise programs.
- Talk about body-image issues with close friends and family.
- Don't criticize people for gaining weight.
- Don't compliment people for losing weight.
- Encourage family and friends to question cultural attitudes about weight and body shape.

Fat and Fit? The Obesity Question

Many people have been taught to fear fat, which leads to unhealthy dieting and intense struggles to lose weight. This thinking is based on the assumption that being fat is unhealthy and should therefore be avoided at all costs.

Now, however, many researchers are questioning the idea that being fat automatically puts a person at risk for health problems. The *New England Journal of Medicine* published an article in 1998, edited by Jerome P. Kassirer, M.D. and Marcia Angell, M.D., that confirms what many researchers have already suspected: treatments for obesity do not work, obesity treatments pose serious health risks, and the treatments are not justified because the health risks of obesity are not as high as once thought.

Some researchers claim that obesity is dangerous to one's health when combined with a sedentary (non-active) lifestyle. It is possible to be fat and healthy. In fact, how healthy a person is depends more on how much a per-

THE NATIONAL ASSOCIATION TO ADVANCE FAT ACCEPTANCE

The National Association to Advance Fat Acceptance (NAAFA) was founded in 1969. Its mission is to work to better the lives of fat people around the world. Through advocacy and education, the organization tries to eliminate the discrimination that fat people face in their lives. NAAFA also works to empower fat people and help them accept their bodies and live more fulfilling lives.

NAAFA's basic message is that a person's worth should not be based on his or her body size. NAAFA uses the word "fat" in the hopes that people will stop using it as an insult and remember it is just an adjective (descriptive word). In this way, the word will not cause shame or embarrassment.

The organization challenges ideas about the connection between obesity and health risks. It promotes research that accurately studies the different aspects of being fat. The goal is to move away from looking for ways to help fat people lose weight and, instead, help fat people be healthy.

NAAFA has more than fifty chapters across the United States that provide support groups for people to share their feelings. Since being fat can be emotionally painful and isolating in many societies, especially in the United States, the organization promotes programs that unite people with similar experiences.

son exercises rather than how much a person weighs. Weight alone is not a proper indication of how healthy a person is, and it is more beneficial for a person to concentrate on fitness instead of fatness.

FOR MORE INFORMATION

Books

Bode, Janet. *Food Fight: A Guide to Eating Disorders for Pre-Teens and Their Parents.* New York: Simon and Schuster, 1997.

Cooke, Kaz. *Real Gorgeous: The Truth About Body and Beauty.* New York: W.W. Norton, 1996.

Hornbacher, Marya. *Wasted: A Memoir of Anorexia and Bulimia.* New York: HarperCollins, 1998.

Kolodny, Nancy. *When Food's a Foe: How You Can Confront and Conquer Your Eating Disorder.* Boston: Little Brown & Co., 1992.

Krasnow, Michael. *My Life as a Male Anorexic.* New York: Haworth Press, 1996.

Sacker, Ira M. *Dying to Be Thin: Understanding and Defeating Anorexia Nervosa and Bulimia—A Practical Lifesaving Guide.* Warner Books, 1987.

Web sites

Eating Disorders Information. [Online] http://eatingdisorders.about.com (Accessed November 1, 1999).

14

Habits and Behaviors

A habit is defined as a way of behaving that is repeated so often it no longer involves conscious thought. A habit might be a person brushing her teeth every night before bed, or walking the dog every morning before school or work. These habits would typically be considered "good" habits to have because they are of benefit to the person performing them. Other kinds of habits might be a person stealing one item from a department store every time he visits the store, or drinking alcohol every weekend at a friend's house. These habits would typically be considered "bad" habits because they may bring harm to the person performing them.

Another definition of habit is an addiction. Both good and bad habits can be addictive in nature. When someone eats a favorite cereal for breakfast every morning, that person has established a good habit because it is important to eat breakfast every day. If, though, the person became so dependent on eating a particular brand of cereal every morning that his mood changed for the worse if he was unable to eat the cereal one morning, his habit would be more serious. One could argue that he was addicted to the cereal. Of course one can't become physically addicted to a brand of cereal the way one can become physically addicted, for example, to the nicotine in cigarettes, but this does serve as an example of how a habit can sometimes turn in to a dangerous behavior.

This chapter will focus on several types of negative habits and behaviors and ways to treat them. From drugs and alcohol to internet addiction and gambling, these habits pose potentially life-threatening risks to all who partake of them.

ADDICTION

Addiction is most commonly defined as dependence on harmful, habit-forming drugs (although drugs do not always have to be the object of the addiction). When most people think of the word addiction, they conjure images of a world they expect never to know. They imagine emaciated heroin addicts in dark alleys or remember rock stars long dead from overdoses. Addiction doesn't always look as menacing as public-service announcements or after-school television programs depict it to be. In fact, many people come into contact with some kind of addiction every day or are addicted to some substance they might consider benign (harmless). While addiction is com-

WORDS TO KNOW

Addiction: The state of needing to compulsively repeat a behavior.

Altered consciousness: A state of awareness that is different from typical, waking consciousness; often induced with the use of drugs and alcohol.

Benign: Harmless; also, non-cancerous.

Compulsive behavior: Behavior that is repeated over and over again, uncontrollably.

Crash: Coming down from being high on drugs or alcohol.

Cut: The habit of mixing illegal drugs with another substance to produce a greater quantity of that substance.

Delirium: Mental disturbance marked by confusion, disordered speech, and even hallucinations.

Dependent: A reliance on something or someone.

Detoxification: The process of freeing an individual of an intoxicating or addictive substance in the body or to free from dependence.

Euphoric: Having the feeling of well-being or elation.

Genetic: Something inherited through one's genes.

Habit: A behavior or routine that is repeated.

Hallucination: The illusion of seeing or hearing something that does not really exist.

Hangover: The syndrome that occurs after being high on drugs or drinking alcohol, often including nausea, headache, dizziness, and fuzzy-mindedness.

Inhalants: Substances that people sniff to get high.

Kleptomania: Habitual stealing.

Mantra: A phrase repeated during meditation to center the mind.

Meditation: A practice that helps one to center and focus the mind; sometimes used to help recovering addicts.

Overdose: A dangerous, often deadly, reaction to taking too much of a certain drug.

Perception: One's consciousness and way of observing things.

Predisposition: To be susceptible to something.

Prohibition: An era in the 1920s when alcohol was made illegal.

Psychoactive: Something that affects brain function, mood and behavior.

Psychological vulnerability: Used to describe individuals who are potential candidates for drug addiction because of prior experiences or other influences.

Pyromania: Habitual need to start fires.

Ritual: Observances or ceremonies that mark change, renewal, or other events.

Self-medicate: When a person treats an ailment, mental or physical, with alcohol or drugs rather than seeing a physician or mental health professional.

Synthetic: Human-made; not occurring in nature.

Tolerance: The build-up of resistance to the effects of a substance.

Withdrawal: The phase of removal of drugs or alcohol from the system of the user.

mon, becoming addicted to a substance or an activity can have serious consequences. And it's not something that just happens to "other" people.

Many adults, and an increasing number of teenagers, drink coffee first thing every morning. In fact, many people feel that without their first cup, normal daily functioning seems impossible. This reflects the problem inherent to addiction—the need itself. The subject of the addiction may seem harmless or even healthy (such as exercise addiction), but too much of anything can be dangerous. Having a cup of coffee once in a while because it tastes good is not a problem; however, caffeine (the addictive substance in coffee) addiction can eventually make people sick.

In the case of alcoholics (those addicted to alcohol), many feel that they must have a drink before they can socialize. Similarly, sugar addicts cannot go for very long without eating something sweet. In fact, they can get depressed, anxious, and irritable when deprived of sugar. Addictions of all types, whether they are to hard drugs, such as heroin, or everyday substances, such as caffeine or sugar, can disrupt a person's life and ruin his or her mental and physical well-being. Addiction to drugs and alcohol, because they are mind-altering substances, poses more of a direct threat to the user than do substances that don't immediately change one's perception.

Dependence

Addiction is dependence on something or someone. Infants, for example, are dependent on their parents for sustenance and other basic needs, such as shelter. Addicted people are dependent on a substance to function normally and feel good. Addicts are scared of the consequences of separation from their substance of choice. Addicted people exist at many levels of functioning and degrees of healing. There are addicts in all walks of life, from physicians and attorneys to schoolteachers and actors. Some of these individuals are able to perform their jobs without anyone else becoming aware of a problem. They are able to fool others into thinking they can function normally. For other individuals, however, their addictions prevent them from holding onto a job or even engaging in activities with family and friends.

Whatever the case, whatever a person's level of functioning, to truly heal, addicts need to admit to themselves that they need help. Healing from addiction is a process of really taking a good look at one's own self. Self-examination can be quite intimidating, and many people would rather avoid it and hide in drinking, drugging or codependence. Self-discovery means not only uncovering the positive attributes a person may not be aware of; it also means coming to terms with shortcomings, flaws, and inadequacies and learning to accept those things.

Learning about the different forms of addiction and tools for healing can help those suffering from it. These coping strategies can help friends and family of people with addictions, too.

Most people who use drugs are seeking an altered state of consciousness. The need to alter consciousness is not a new phenomenon. Historical evidence shows that people of all cultures and eras have experimented with mind-altering substances, both natural and synthetic (human-made or artificial). People who use drugs seek to make the world around them look and feel different. This might mean trying to make a bleak life seem better or simply more interesting.

Drugs often make people feel powerful. That's why taking drugs is called "getting high." Drugs endow a user with a false sense of power that, of course, recedes when the artificial high ends. Addiction occurs when a person compulsively attempts to continue that high by taking a drug over and over again.

People use drugs for many, many reasons. For example, adolescents have reported that they experimented with marijuana to enhance sexuality; to feel more confident; for pleasure and relaxation; to make themselves more comfortable in social situations; to understand themselves better; for acceptance by their peers or to achieve elevated social status; to defy authority; and to expand their minds.

There are many theories governing an individual's choice to use drugs when others do not. Initial experimentation and addiction are two very different behaviors, though. The reason many people continue to seek out drugs after their first use is, again, an attempt to reproduce the same pleasure and an altered state of consciousness initially achieved the first time a certain drug was used. The second time and each instance thereafter, a user is trying to recapture the intensity of that first experience. Ultimately, these feelings cannot be replicated, and this is where an addiction starts. Drug users in search of that elusive pleasure will continue to search for the feelings inspired by their first time, even if all the consecutive uses affect them adversely; this is particularly dangerous with crack cocaine. (Many drug experts suggest that the initial experience of using crack cocaine is so intense that it takes only one use to kick-start an addiction.) Furthermore, over time, addicts' bodies develop

Actor/comedian Chris Farley died as a result of a drug overdose at the age of 33. (UPI/Corbis-Bettmann. Reproduced by permission.)

a tolerance for a drug, meaning they will eventually have to take more and more of their drug of choice each time they use in order to achieve the same high.

Addiction counselors and others who work with substance abusers consider drug use and abuse to be a self-destructive behavior. According to this model, the user may not be consciously aware of being deeply depressed and engaging in self-destructive activities. Psychoanalytic counselors (see Chapter 15: Mental Health Therapies) also interpret drug abuse as a form of suicidal behavior. Proponents of psychoanalysis believe that an addict is usually unaware of his or her deep-rooted problems, and the addiction is a symptom of unreleased pain resulting from these buried problems.

Causes of Substance Abuse

There isn't one single cause that lies at the root of drug addiction. This is why drug addiction is so very hard to understand and treat. Several years ago a term called "addictive personality" became very popular in the media. Those in the drug and alcohol field dislike this term because they consider it overly simplistic and unfair to addicts. It implies that drug abusers are to blame for their illness because they have a defective personality. A better term to describe a person's predisposition to drug abuse might be psychological (mind-related) vulnerability. This means that the addict had some prior psychological factor that made a pattern of substance abuse more likely to begin.

For example, people who have mood disorders (see Chapter 12: Mental Illness) sometimes self-medicate (make themselves feel better or more in balance) by using drugs. There are a number of personality traits that are thought to be shared by drug abusers (and alcoholics, too). These traits include high emotionality; anxiety; immaturity in relationships; low frustration tolerance; inability to express anger; problems with authority; low self-esteem; perfectionism; compulsiveness; feelings of isolation; sex-role confusion; depression; hostility; and sexual immaturity. Stress is also thought to be a factor contributing to drug abuse. This is not referring to run-of-the-mill, everyday stress from work or school, but the kind of stress that is the result of traumatic experiences, such as the sudden loss of a loved one. Stress in early

LOST TO DRUGS

Many actors and musicians have waged well-documented battles with addiction, whether it be to drugs or alcohol. Some have come out triumphant, such as Drew Barrymore, who battled alcoholism at a very young age, and Matthew Perry, who triumphed over an addiction to painkillers. Unfortunately, though, many talented individuals have lost their lives to drugs. In the early 1970s, the world of rock-and-roll mourned the overdose deaths of three musical giants, Jimi Hendrix, Janis Joplin, and Jim Morrison. In recent years, Shannon Hoon, lead singer of the rock group Blind Melon, died of a heroin overdose. Hollywood has lost its share of beloved performers as well. Actress Judy Garland, who played Dorothy in *The Wizard of Oz,* died in 1969 of an overdose from drugs as did actor River Phoenix in 1995 at the age of 23. In 1997, comedian Chris Farley, age 33, died of a drug overdose as well, following in the footsteps of his own idol, actor/comedian John Belushi, who overdosed in 1982 also at the age of 33.

childhood, such as having been sexually or physically abused, can also lead to drug abuse.

A sense of self is one of the most important factors in the potential for drug addiction. A person with a strong sense of self will have several obvious qualities. One will have a sense of one's own individuality and be aware of talents and a place in the world. Also, one will be able to begin, develop, and complete projects and to coexist comfortably in different types of relationships. Those with a weak sense of self are more likely to seek out drugs as way of giving them a sense of self, which quickly vanishes once the drug wears off.

According to addiction counselors and researchers, preventing substance abuse in kids is more about giving them something to live for and helping them to foster a strong sense of self rather than keeping them away from what is deemed as the dangerous and enticing world of drugs.

Families and Drug Abuse

Family history of drug abuse is another risk factor for potential substance abusers. Some experts theorize that human beings may possess a genetic predisposition to drug dependence. But a poorly functioning family system may contribute to the development of an addiction just as powerfully. Children of alcoholics and drug abusers are more likely to develop their own addictions later in life. However, it remains unclear as to whether this development is a result of nature (inherited biologically) or nurture (environmental factors, such as a person's family relations and social environment).

Adolescence, specifically, is a time of change and risk. Because teens are just beginning to develop their fragile sense of self, they are more prone to fall victim to drug abuse. This vulnerability is heightened because teens are exploring identity, social skills, and independence. Peer pressure, the need to fit in and be liked, often causes teens to experiment with drugs. If a teen is at a party and everyone around is partying, one might feel compelled to take a drink or smoke cigarettes or use marijuana. Usually these situations do not occur as they do in the movies, where other kids actually pressure their peers; rather, peer pressure tends to work in more subtle ways. If a teen is feeling left out and alone at a party, he or she might believe that joining others in smoking a marijuana cigarette will help in latching onto a group of friends. This is a reflection of teens' needs to feel as though they are part of a group—that they belong.

SHARING NEEDLES

Injecting drugs (using drugs by shooting them directly in to a vein with a needle) carries an even more deadly threat to the body than administering them in other ways, such as smoking or snorting. Heroin addicts, and others, who shoot drugs and share needles are in one of the highest risk groups for infection with hepatitis and human immunodeficiency virus (HIV), which can lead to acquired immune deficiency syndrome (AIDS). HIV and hepatitis are transferred from person to person via bodily fluids. If the blood from an infected person is transferred to another person via a dirty needle, that person is at great risk for contracting these life-threatening diseases.

A teen feeling like the odd one out might even turn to doing drugs in private as a way to escape the pain of loneliness. Since drugs and alcohol are often easily available to teens, and avoiding contact with them is often difficult, many teens will have encounters with substance abuse either with themselves or someone they know. Willpower and a strong sense of self seem to be the only things that keep people, in general, away from the trap of substance abuse and addiction.

DEPRESSANTS

Depressants are the family of substances that slow down, or depress, bodily functions. They tend to make the user sleepy or sluggish. The following drugs fall in to the category of depressants.

Narcotics

Narcotics include opiates, the class of drugs derived from the poppy plant. Opiates have been used for thousands of years in Asia both for pleasure and medicinal uses. Natural opiates include morphine, codeine, and heroin. Synthetic opiates include codeine, oxycodone, and meperidine. They cause a wide variety of effects and side effects, such as pain relief, euphoria, respiratory depression, drowsiness, constriction of the pupils, nausea and vomiting, itching, and constipation. Narcotics tend to be easily addictive when used regularly because of their quick and powerful effects.

Narcotics can be ingested, injected, snorted or smoked. When opiates are smoked, it takes just five seconds for the drug to reach the brain. If a person addicted to narcotics is without that drug for even four to six hours after the narcotic use stops, he or she can feel the beginnings of withdrawal.

TOLERANCE TO NARCOTICS. Tolerance (the ability to resist the effects of something) develops quickly with the use of narcotics. Users must take more and more of the drug to get back to the desired effect. This can lead to overdose. Detoxification (cleansing the body of a toxic substance) is necessary for the user if one wants to

Heroin addiction is one of the most difficult and painful addictions to overcome. (Custom Medical Stock Photo. Reproduced by permission.)

return to a normal life. In order to detoxify and cleanse the body of the drug, withdrawal must occur. Withdrawal is the experience of ridding one's body of any substance it has become accustomed to. Withdrawal from opiates can cause the following symptoms: appetite suppression; nausea and vomiting; dilated pupils; gooseflesh; restlessness; intestinal spasm; abdominal pain; muscle spasms; kicking movements (reason for the expression, "kicking the habit"); diarrhea; increased heart rate and blood pressure; chills, hot flushes and sweating; irritability; insomnia; violent yawning; severe sneezing and runny nose; crying and tearing, nasal inflammation; and depressive moods and tremors. Medical treatment is sometimes sought because of extreme weight loss, dehydration, body chemistry disturbances, and stress on the heart. Without treatment, withdrawal symptoms can last from seven to ten days.

> **IT IS IMPORTANT TO REMEMBER THAT EVEN IF A DOCTOR PRESCRIBES A DRUG FOR SOMEONE, THAT PERSON CAN ABUSE THE DRUG AND BECOME ADDICTED TO IT.**

Anti-anxiety Drugs and Sleep Aids

Barbiturates and benzodiazepines are in the sedative-hypnotic class of drugs and are usually prescribed by doctors for anxiety disorders (see Chapter 12: Mental Illness) or to induce sleep, although benzodiazepines are prescribed more often because they are safer. (It is important to remember that even if a doctor prescribes a drug for someone, that person can abuse the drug and become addicted to it.) In the 1960s and 1970s barbiturates began to seep into the black market (that is, they were being sold on the street without a doctor's prescription). Prescription names for barbiturates are Amobarbital, Pentobarbital, Butubarbital, Phenobarbital, Secobarbital, and Pento-secobarbital.

Anti-anxiety drugs and sleep aids are taken orally, in pill form. They cause drowsiness, relaxation, and a sense of well-being. Effects are similar to those of alcohol. If used over any extended period of time, barbiturates can cause extreme physical and psychological dependence. Tolerance to the euphoric effects occur quickly, so more and more must be used to develop the desired effect. Withdrawal causes dizziness, weakness, sleeplessness, anxiety, tremors, nausea, vomiting, delirium, delusions, and hallucinations.

Overdose is common with these types of drugs. In fact, they are often the drugs of choice

DRUGS: IN THE MEDICINE CABINET AND ON THE STREET

Psychoactive drugs are those that affect brain functions, mood and behavior. Non-psychoactive drugs are substances that in normal doses do not directly affect the brain. There are several different categories of psychoactive drugs. There are both over-the-counter and prescription drugs that fall into the category of psychoactive agents so people should be aware that so-called street drugs (such as marijuana, heroin or cocaine) aren't the only drugs that cause addiction. It's important to remember that the effects of any drug depend on several variables. They are the amount taken at one time, the user's past drug experience, the method of administration (how the drug is taken—inhaled, smoked, swallowed, etc.), and the circumstances under which the drug is taken.

for people wanting to commit suicide. Symptoms of overdose are severe mood alteration; confusion and disorientation; slurred speech; impaired motor co-ordination; involuntary rapid eye movement from side to side; dilated pupils; and respiratory depression.

There are other drugs with barbiturate-like effects that are not classified as barbiturates, such as methaqualone, better known by the trade name Quaaludes, or the street name ludes. Quaaludes were thought to be a nonaddictive alternative to barbiturates when they were introduced in the 1960s. They turned out to have high abuse potential. They're very popular with college and high school students and have been illegal since 1984. They are often mixed with alcohol, creating a deadly combination. They produce sedation and sleep. Methoqualone induces headaches, hangovers, fatigue, dizziness, drowsiness, menstrual disturbances, dry mouth, nosebleeds, diarrhea, skin eruptions, numbness, and pain in the arms and legs. Eight to twenty grams can produce severe toxicity, coma, and death. Tolerance builds quickly, and withdrawal is much like detoxification from barbiturates.

Marijuana

Cannabis sativa is the plant that is used to produce both marijuana and hashish. Marijuana is the unprocessed, dried leaves, flowers, seeds, and stems of the plant. Hashish is stronger, and made from the resin (liquidy substance) in the plant. THC is the strongest psychoactive compound found in cannabis. There are many street names for marijuana: pot, grass, weed, bud, kind bud,

MEDICAL MARIJUANA

Native Americans have used marijuana medicinally for thousands of years. Since it was made illegal in the United States, the use of marijuana for medical reasons has been extremely controversial. Extensive research has been done about the use of THC to treat people undergoing chemotherapy (a cancer treatment). It has been proven that THC is the best cure for the nausea and vomiting associated with this type of cancer treatment. There has also been research in the area of using medical marijuana as a treatment for the pain of glaucoma (an eye disease) and the wasting syndrome (chronic weight loss and the inability to substantially gain weight once it sets in) associated with AIDS. Less researched, but still potentially useful, is the use of marijuana for asthma relief, spasm relief, and anxiety reduction, and relief of alcohol withdrawal symptoms.

As of 1998, thirty-four states had statutes on the books allowing derivatives (substances obtained from) of marijuana to be used in research and/or treatment. In 1996, Arizona passed Proposition 200 and California passed Proposition 215, effectively legalizing the use of medical marijuana. Although the use of medical marijuana has proven to have few side effects and tremendous benefits for ailing individuals, it is still a hugely controversial topic because of the illegality of "street" marijuana. However, the National Institute of Health (NIH) now supports the use of medical marijuana, and there is a group called National Organization for the Reform of Marijuana Laws (NORML) that organizes and lobbies in favor of changing the laws forbidding the use of medical marijuana, but they haven't been able to garner enough support to counter the anti-medical marijuana groups.

herb, and reefer. The cigarettes used to roll and smoke the drug are sometimes called doobies, joints, spliffs, fatties, roaches or blunts. Marijuana can
also be smoked in a pipe, or a water pipe, called a bong. Pot is the most
widely used illicit drug.

The effects of pot often depend on the potency (strength) of the drug.
The strength of marijuana has increased tremendously since the 1960s. The
common effects of pot smoking are feelings of exhilaration, increased appetite
(the "munchies"), relaxation and giddiness (including uncontrollable laugh-
ter), increase in heart rate, drowsiness, dry mouth and tongue (referred to as
"cotton mouth"), impaired short-term memory, altered perception of time and
space, dilated pupils, and paranoia (irrational fear for one's safety). The long-
term adverse effects of marijuana are still unknown. Psychological dependence
on the drug is common. Regular users begin to depend on smoking pot to
relax, and even to sleep. Habitual users often smoke pot immediately upon
awakening.

Withdrawal from pot can cause irritability, decreased appetite, sleep disturbances, sweating, nausea and diarrhea. Hang-
overs are common the day after smoking pot.
They are different from hangovers after drinking
alcohol, however. Pot hangovers cause dizziness
and inability to concentrate. Chronic (frequent)
use can cause physical dependence. Marijuana is
known to damage the respiratory system and to
suppress the body's immune system. Pot can also
make men infertile (unable to father children),
and interfere with women's menstrual cycles.
Children and teenagers (ages eleven to fifteen)
who begin smoking before they have reached
their full height can suffer stunted growth.

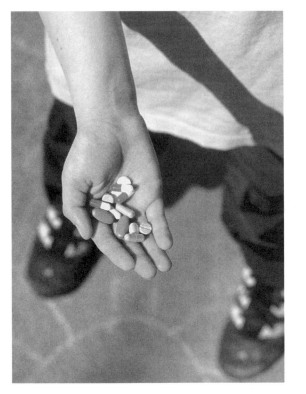

Despite being illegal, many drugs are readily available
on school campuses. (Photograph by Robert J. Huffman.
Field Mark Publications. Reproduced by permission.)

STIMULANTS

Stimulants are the family of substances that
temporarily speed up or excite the function of
the body or one of its parts. They tend to make
the user unusually excited or overactive. The following drugs fall in to the category of stimulants.

Amphetamines

Amphetamines are central nervous system
stimulants that give the user a temporary feeling
of energy. A popular nickname for amphetamines
is "uppers" because they make the user feel up

and wide awake. Amphetamines have been prescribed by doctors for a wide variety of ailments for years. Dieters have used amphetamines for many years, in prescription and over-the-counter form. They have been prescribed by doctors for obesity, depression, and narcolepsy (uncontrolled fits of sleep). Ritalin is a drug in the amphetamine family that is still prescribed for hyperactive children. In the 1970s there was a crisis of abuse of amphetamines. People began injecting them intravenously (directly into veins). These individuals were called "speed-freaks" (speed is one of the street names for amphetamines). Doctors responded to this crisis by limiting the amount of prescriptions for amphetamines. Nonprescription, over-the-counter versions of amphetamines are used every day by, for example, college students cramming for exams and truck drivers attempting to stay awake for long drives.

Therapeutic doses of amphetamines stimulate the central nervous system, increase blood pressure, widen the pupils, quicken the breath, lower appetite, and decrease fatigue. Higher doses can cause agitation, blurred vision, tremors, and heart palpitations. Severe reactions can result in dilated pupils, sweating, cramps, nausea, heart problems, hypertension, panic, aggressive and violent behavior, hallucinations, delirium, high fevers, convulsions and seizures. People have died from amphetamine abuse because of burst blood vessels, heart attacks and high fevers. Physical dependence to moderate doses of amphetamines is highly unusual, but psychological dependence from even low doses is common. Chronic users of amphetamines have long-term health consequences.

Methamphetamines

Methamphetamine is a newer class of illegal amphetamine. Some street names for it are meth, ice, zip, go-fast, cristy, and chalk. When meth is mixed with water and injected with a needle it is called crank. Sometimes crank is mixed with crack cocaine. The mixture is called "croak."

Often meth and certain so-called designer drugs (see section below) are cut (mixed or diluted) with cocaine or heroin. Sometimes they are cut with cornstarch, baby laxatives, baking soda, or even rat poison. Meth is even more dangerous than the typical, older forms of amphetamines because it gets into the system faster, lasts longer, and can have even more deadly effects.

Cocaine

Cocaine is another central nervous system stimulant. It comes from the coca plant, found

CLUBS AND DRUGS

The newest form of methamphetamine is a very pure version that is smoked in a pipe. In this form, the drug looks like little chips of ice. For that reason, it has picked up the nicknames ice, glass, or crystal. Meth is often used by ravers, kids that go to all-night parties that take place in empty warehouses and clubs. Raves are parties where electronic music is played and drugs such as meth, acid (LSD, or lysergic acid diethylamide) and ecstasy (MDMA, or methylenedioxymethamphetamine) are common and easily available. Kids who want to stay awake and dance until the sunrise (and often beyond) often use meth. Lokers (another name for people who smoke meth) can be identified by their hyper-energized, artificial dance moves.

in South America. (The soft drink Coca-Cola originally contained extracts of the coca leaf.) Some street names for cocaine are blow, C, coke, and snow. It is usually snorted. At one time, cocaine was very expensive, and only the very wealthy could buy it. In the 1980s, it became much more affordable and was considered the "drug of choice" among young, successful professionals. Crack is a smokable form of cocaine that is much more potent (strong), cheaper and sold in rocks. Crack is highly addictive; some experts say even one use has the potential to make someone addicted.

Cocaine causes an initial euphoric high that can last from fifteen to thirty minutes. People on cocaine tend to talk a mile a minute and feel like they are invincible. Socially awkward people on cocaine jump out of their shells and act tremendously self-confident, often arrogant. A cocaine user may feel sexually stimulated at first, but as the drug wears off this usually doesn't last.

The high from cocaine is short-lived, and "crashing" quickly sets in. A person crashing from a cocaine high is usually depressed, paranoid, irritable, and extremely tired. Because the high is so brief, cocaine users tend to buy a large amount of the drug and go through it quickly. Cocaine has the reputation of being a social drug, and people tend to do it with groups in bars and clubs. For serious users, cocaine binges can last for days. On a binge, a user will snort cocaine every half-hour for days on end. They will live without sleep or food until they crash from exhaustion.

Cocaine is highly addicting, although it is not physically addictive in the way that narcotics, such as heroin, can be. That is, physical tolerance to cocaine does not develop. Rather, users need to take it again and again to avoid crashing. One-time use of cocaine can result in death.

PCP

PCP (phencyclidine) is considered a stimulant although it is not commonly thought of as such. Also known as angel dust, it usually looks like white or colored chunks, powder or crystals. It's often smoked. Low doses produce muscle stiffness and poor coordination, slurred speech, drowsiness, confusion, numbness of the arms and legs, profuse sweating, nausea, vomiting, flushing and increased heart rate. Strange and violent behavior can result from higher doses. In some cases effects from PCP have lasted

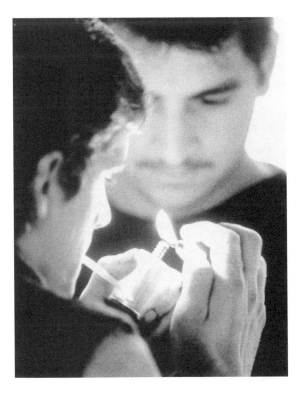

Crack is a smokable form of cocaine that is much stronger, cheaper and sold in rocks. (Photograph by Roy Morsch. Stock Market. Reproduced by permission.)

up to ten weeks. Heavy users can experience deep anxiety, depression and psychotic symptoms.

HALLUCINOGENS

Hallucinogens or psychedelics were the most popular class of drugs in the 1960s. Timothy Leary (1920–1996), a doctor from Harvard University, coined the phrase, "Tune in, turn on, drop out," encouraging young people everywhere to experiment with psychedelics. Hallucinogens affect people by distorting reality, and, at higher doses, often cause hallucinations (the illusion of seeing or hearing something that doesn't really exist). (Other drugs, even alcohol and marijuana, can cause hallucinations, too.)

Synthetic hallucinogens are LSD (lysergic acid diethylamide), mescaline (peyote), and DOM and STP (2,5-dimethoxy-4methylamphetamine), an amphetamine derivative. LSD is also called acid. The synthetic hallucinogens are manufactured in underground laboratories that exist only to serve the illegal drug market. Natural hallucinogens include mescaline, or peyote (this can also be synthetically produced), morning glory seeds, and psilocybin mushrooms (these are often called "shrooms" or "magic mushrooms"; they are not the kind of mushrooms found in supermarkets).

The slang term for taking hallucinogens is "tripping." The experience an individual can have on psychedelics varies widely. The emotional and mental state of the user at the time of "dropping" or taking the drug sets the tone for the trip. If the individual has any feelings of doubt or fear, the drug often exaggerates these emotions. This can cause a nightmarish experience, called a "bad trip." Trips can last anywhere from four to twenty-four hours depending on dosage and circumstances.

LSD. LSD can be taken in different forms. Because it is highly potent, only small amounts are necessary. It is sometimes produced in pill form. More commonly, sheets of LSD called blotter paper are produced. The user puts a tiny piece of the sheet in his or her mouth. These pieces are called dots, tabs or doses. Sometimes acid is taken in liquid form.

The effects of LSD are usually felt within an hour. Physical effects include increased blood pressure, dilated pupils, rapid heartbeat, muscular weakness, trembling, nausea, chills, and hyperventilation. (Sometimes LSD is mixed with amphetamines, and the effects match the speedy physical effects of that class of drugs.) Another possible effect of taking LSD is the flashback. Up to a year after the acid trip, users can have hallucinations caused by LSD left in their systems.

MESCALINE. Mescaline is made from the peyote cactus. The heads or "buttons" of the cactus are dried and put into capsules. It is usually taken orally but can be smoked or injected. It is less potent than LSD. Physical effects include dilated pupils, high body temperature, nausea and vomiting, and muscular relaxation. Mental effects include euphoria, heightened sensory perception, hallucinations, and difficulty in thinking. Higher doses can cause headaches, dry skin, hypotension (lowering of the blood pressure), cardiac depression, and slowing of respiration.

Designer Drugs

Designer drugs, called such because they are "designed" in a laboratory, were created in the 1970s by underground chemists attempting to subvert the drug laws of the day. The designer drugs were only a molecule or two different than some of the synthetic drugs then listed as illegal according to the Controlled Substance Act.

MDMA, better known as Ecstasy, is a very popular designer drug. Some street names for Ecstasy are X, E, XTC, Rave or Adam. It's related to amphetamines and mescaline. It's also called the "love drug" or the "hug drug" because it enhances empathy and relatedness. It also causes a positive mood change, a drop in defense mechanisms, and elevated mood. Some of the negative effects of Ecstasy are the potential for overdosing, extreme fatigue, dilated pupils, dry mouth and throat, tension in the lower jaw, grinding of the teeth and overstimulation. It can also cause extreme paranoia and panic that call for emergency care.

Special K is one of the newer, deadlier designer drugs. It is actually ketamine hydrochloride, a drug widely used as an animal tranquilizer by veterinarians during pet surgery. It is a very powerful hallucinogen. Special K is usually snorted, but it is sometimes sprinkled on tobacco or marijuana cigarettes and smoked. Special K is frequently used in combination with other drugs, such as Ecstasy, heroin and cocaine.

Those high on Special K can enter a "K-hole" and never come out of it. Users describe the "K-hole" as a space where profound hallucinations may occur that include visual distortions and a lost sense of time, sense and identity. Some report experiencing total temporary paralysis (loss of the ability to move or feel sensation). Because users generally become unable to speak or even see what is happening around them, it is not a social drug. One of the other dangers of Special

GHB

GHB (gamma-hydroxybutyrate), an unpredictable, often deadly, designer drug has recently become popular with young adults. It has been used for euphoric, sedative, and anabolic (body building) effects, and is available in liquid or powder forms. Users report it induces a state of relaxation. Known as "liquid ecstacy," "Georgia Home Boy," "scoop," or "grievous bodily harm," GHB, taken alone or with other drugs (such as alcohol), can depress the central nervous system. Serious side effects include: coma, seizures, vomiting, tremors, dizziness, and difficulty breathing or respiratory arrest.

GHB is odorless and colorless with a slightly salty taste. This makes it easy to slip into someone's drink without detection (for this reason, GHB has reportedly been used in cases of date rape). Due to the unpredictable nature of the drug, there is little difference between a dose that will get a person high and one that will kill. Experts agree that there is no safe level of use of GHB.

K is that it's hard to determine that the dosage one has bought from a dealer is authentic. Like some of the other designer drugs, Special K is often cut with other drugs and poisonous agents.

INHALANTS

Inhalants are products that people sniff to get high. The sniffing of glue, solvents, aerosols, cleaning agents, gas from dessert topping sprays, and other gases is common. Because common, everyday products found in most homes and grocery stores can be used as inhalants, sniffing, also called huffing, is popular with teens and others who don't have money or access to buy illegal drugs. People who use inhalants are sometimes referred to as "huffers."

Sniffing is a deadly habit that gained much notoriety in the 1990s, although the practice existed before then. Because the inhalants are legal, everyday products, many teens do not view sniffing as being as harmful as doing "hard" drugs. This is a dangerous and untrue belief. Symptoms of inhalant use are slurred speech, mental disorientation, headaches, dizziness and weakness, muscle spasms, euphoria, and nystagmus (eye movement from side to side). Some of the more serious adverse effects are nausea and vomiting, confusion, panic, tension, aggressive behavior, and permanent brain damage. At higher doses use of inhalants can cause respiratory depression and eventual unconsciousness, resulting in coma and death. Sniffing can also cause heart failure.

ALCOHOL AND ALCOHOLISM

Alcohol is classified as a central nervous system depressant like barbiturates and tranquilizers. Although it is legal for those of a certain age in the United States to use, it is still very much a drug. It is, however, a socially acceptable drug, unlike some of the drugs already discussed. After tobacco use, alcohol is the most widely used psychoactive drug in the world.

Drinking alcohol, whether beer, wine, or liquor, causes a vast array of effects. Even small amounts of alcohol impair drinkers so much that they cannot perform simple motor tasks. Every tissue in the human body is affected by alcohol consumption. Individual effects of drinking vary. Body weight and size, gender, metabolism, the amount of alcohol consumed at the time, and the type and amount of food in the stomach determine the blood alcohol level. Mild intoxication

Sniffing common household products to get high is a deadly habit. (Custom Medical Stock Photo. Reproduced by permission.)

can cause feelings of warmth, flushed skin, impaired judgment, and decreased inhibitions. Deeper intoxication can cause a slowing of reflexes and more obvious lessening of judgment and inhibitions. Slurred speech, double vision, and memory and comprehension loss can follow.

Eventually drinkers can experience vomiting, incontinence (losing bladder or bowel control), and the inability to stand on their own. Many people pass out when they've had too much to drink. Blackouts are not uncommon. In a blackout, drinkers will not remember large segments of their experiences, even when the story is relayed to them. Coma and death are possible results of excessive drinking. Drinking even a small amount of alcohol can result in a hangover. Hangovers can cause headaches, fatigue, nausea, shakiness, and extreme thirst. (For those who insist on drinking, consuming plenty of water before, during and after will prevent the dehydration that is a consequence of alcohol consumption.)

The dangers of short- and long-term abuse of alcohol are numerous. Short-term abuse can cause the physical reactions described above, plus the possibility of serious hazards incurred by loss of faculties. Drunk driving is the most serious and immediate consequence. Drunk people make impaired decisions that very often cost them their lives and the lives of those they love. The decision to get behind the wheel after drinking can result in drivers having to spend the rest of their lives in prison. Death is the most serious result of driving drunk. People who have been drinking, even those who do not think they are drunk, should never drive no matter the circumstances.

Long-term effects of alcohol abuse are liver diseases, such as cirrhosis and cancer. These are usually fatal. Alcoholics have higher rates of peptic ulcers, pneumonia, cancer of the upper digestive and respiratory tracts, heart and artery disease, tuberculosis and suicide than the rest of the population. Fetal Alcohol Syndrome (FAS) is a condition that drinking mothers pass on to their infants. Pregnant women should not drink alcohol at all. FAS is the leading cause of birth defects.

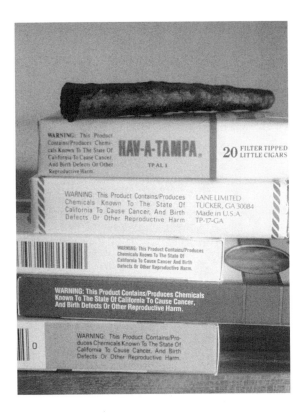

Warning labels are placed on all tobacco products informing users of the dangers of nicotine and smoking. (Photograph by Robert J. Huffman. Field Mark Publications. Reproduced by permission.)

Withdrawal from Alcohol

Six to twelve hours after the last drink, an alcoholic can begin to feel the affects of withdrawal from alcohol. The stage one symptoms are psychomotor agitation, anxiety, insomnia, appetite suppression, stomach problems, elevated heart rate and blood pressure, sweating and tremors. Within twenty-four hours, stage two withdrawal symptoms begin. They include the symptoms of stage one, plus hallucinations and seizures.

NICOTINE

Nicotine is a drug that is legal in the United States for those over the age of eighteen. It is found in tobacco products, most notably cigarettes. Although the law prohibits selling cigarettes to minors, smoking is on the rise among teens. Many people do not think of cigarettes as drugs because they are so popular and socially acceptable. In fact, smoking is the most lethal of all the addictive behaviors. Smoking kills more people each year than AIDS, fires, illegal drugs, and suicides combined. It is best to avoid smoking all together because it is among the most difficult addictions to shake.

Comparison of a smoker's lung (right) to a normal lung (left). (Photograph by A. Glauberman. Photo Researchers Inc. Reproduced by permission.)

Smoking causes coughing, shortness of breath, fatigue, yellow teeth, bad breath, lung cancer, throat and mouth cancer, dry skin, dry hair, emphysema (a chronic lung disease), asthma, and a variety of other problems. At one time, the dangers of nicotine and smoking were not as well known as they are today and smoking was a symbol of "being cool." That era is long gone. And the proven negative effects of smoking are well documented. Many teens start smoking at first because they think it looks cool. But more and more teens are learning how truly not cool smoking is. Pregnant and breast-feeding women face special dangers when it comes to smoking. For example, a fetus exposed to the effects of smoking runs the risk of having a low birth weight.

CAFFEINE

Caffeine is a stimulant found in coffee, some teas, chocolate, some over-the-counter drugs, and cola drinks. Due to the popularity of these products, especially of coffee and cola drinks, caffeine is the most popular drug in the world. It is sometimes used medically, but mostly caffeine is used non-medically for its stimulating effect on mood and behavior. When someone wakes up in the morning and can't get started without a cup of coffee, this is a classic sign of caffeine addiction. People who regularly consume five or more cups of coffee per day develop a tolerance to the drug. An addicted person will suffer headache, irritability, and drowsiness when they do not consume the amount of caffeine to which their body has grown accustomed, due to their physical and psychological dependence on the drug.

SUGAR ADDICTION

Sugar addiction is common among children and adults and is no different, in terms of physical response, than addiction to other substances. Refined white sugar is an ingredient in almost all processed foods found at the supermarket: breakfast cereals, sodas, breads, canned soups, cakes, cookies, ice cream and more. It is in just about everything but raw fruits and vegetables (which contain natural, not refined, sugar). Most people don't think twice about it. But each time the human body consumes sugar it reacts. Insulin (a hormone that regulates the amount of sugar in the blood) in the body rises and energy temporarily shoots up. That is why people sometimes eat candy bars when they need a quick lift. But the problem with the rise in energy is the consequent crash. Once the sugar leaves the system, the sugar-eater gets fatigued and craves more. This causes a cycle of dependence that is hard to break. Because refined white sugar is a food (and because it's hard to avoid unless one really makes an effort) most people do not connect health and emotional problems to sugar addiction (for instance, some hyperactive children can return to normal behavior when taken off sugar). In the long run, too much processed sugar can cause cavities, diabetes, and a host of other illnesses.

TREATMENT FOR ADDICTION

Whether a person is suffering from alcoholism or drug addiction, it is clear that treatment is necessary for successful recovery. Going "cold turkey," the idea of abruptly quitting using a substance without any treatment, only works for a very small minority. Many people believe in the saying "once an addict, always an addict." That is, recovery from addiction is thought to be a lifelong process and not one that stops once an addict initially stops using. Many former addicts who have been substance-free for years still consider themselves in recovery. There are many options and theories about recovery available to addicts who seek help.

Alcoholics Anonymous (AA)

Alcoholics Anonymous is the most famous treatment organization in the world. AA meetings take place just about everywhere in the United States each day and in other countries as well. AA is based on a twelve-step recovery plan. The steps successful members of AA have completed are as follows:

1. We admitted we were powerless over alcohol—that our lives had become unmanageable.

2. Came to believe that a Power greater than ourselves could restore us to sanity.

3. Made a decision to turn our will and our lives over to the care of God, as we understood Him.

4. Made a searching and fearless moral inventory of ourselves.

5. Admitted to God, to ourselves and to another human being the exact nature of our wrongs.

6. Were entirely ready to have God remove all these defects of character.

7. Humbly asked Him to remove our shortcomings.

8. Made a list of all persons we had harmed, and became willing to make amends to them all.

9. Made direct amends to such a people wherever possible, except when to do so would injure them or others.

10. Continued to take personal inventory, and when we were wrong, promptly admitted it.

11. Sought through prayer and meditation to improve our conscious contact with God, as we understood Him, praying only for knowledge of His will for us and the power to carry that out.

12. Having had a spiritual awakening as the result of these steps, we tried to carry this message to alcoholics and to practice these principles in all our affairs.

These steps have been modified and used by many other recovery programs for all different types of addictions. AA is a plan for self-reflection and taking responsibility. Some people are uncomfortable with the word God, and the reference to God as a Him. Those individuals can substitute other words for any spiritual language, and the steps can still work for them.

Abstinence from all alcohol is a requirement for those in AA. New members are given a sponsor, a recovering alcoholic (called such because many former alcoholics feel they are always in recovery) who can lead them through the process. The sponsor stands by to assist the new members. If they feel they might relapse (that is, return to drinking), they are told to call their sponsor right away for guidance.

Methadone Maintenance

Methadone maintenance is a popular treatment for heroin addicts. Methadone is a substitute drug for heroin. It is prescribed and distributed in a controlled environment. It helps to alleviate the severe symptoms of withdrawal from heroin, without enforcing abstinence. The goal of methadone maintenance is to wean a heroin addict from heroin and then, ultimately, from methadone, which does not have as severe withdrawal symptoms as does heroin. Widespread HIV infection among heroin addicts (from sharing dirty needles) increased the acceptance of methadone maintenance as a treatment for addiction in the United States. (European countries have used this treatment for years without problem.)

TAKE THE QUIZ

On its web site (http://www. alcoholics-anonymous.org) Alcoholics Anonymous has a questionnaire for teens. If teens take the quiz and answer even one question with a "yes," they are directed to explore whether they might have a serious problem with alcohol.

A Simple 12-Question Quiz Designed To Help You Decide

1. Do you drink because you have problems? To relax?

2. Do you drink when you get mad at other people, your friends or parents?

3. Do you prefer to drink alone, rather than with others?

4. Are your grades starting to slip? Are you goofing off on your job?

5. Did you ever try to stop drinking or drink less—and fail?

6. Have you begun to drink in the morning, before school or work?

7. Do you gulp your drinks?

8. Do you ever have loss of memory due to your drinking?

9. Do you lie about your drinking?

10. Do you ever get into trouble when you're drinking?

11. Do you get drunk when you drink, even when you don't mean to?

12. Do you think it's cool to be able to hold your liquor?

Intervention

Intervention is a popular mode of treatment for addiction and other negative behavioral problems. Intervention is an organized visit upon the afflicted individual by friends and loved ones. Often a counselor is present and counselors almost always help in planning the meeting. The intervention is designed to confront the addicted individual in a nonjudgmental fashion. The group offers caring, guidance, and love to the person being confronted. The group tells the individual that they are aware of the addiction and that they care for the person and want him or her to seek help and get better. Often an intervention helps addicts realize that their addiction is not a secret and that they are affecting their loved ones' lives. An intervention also sometimes backfires and causes the subject of the intervention to become immediately defensive and storm out of the meeting. That is why taking this approach needs to be considered very carefully and should involve a trained substance abuse counselor (see Chapter 7: Health Care Careers for information on substance abuse counselors).

Other Treatment Considerations

Anyone suffering from addiction and attempting to recover will experience a certain degree of pain and discomfort. The person must believe that kicking the habit is worth it, though, and be willing to ride out the discomfort to reach sobriety. While this is much easier said than done, there are some tools that recovering addicts can use to make the road to recovery a little smoother.

It makes sense for all people to eat right and get a healthy amount of sleep, but for those that have been abusing their bodies with a substance, healthy eating is even more important. Vitamin C can be of great help in flushing the toxic substance out of the system. It cleanses the tissues. Essential fatty acids, such as those found in flax oil (this can be found at the health food store), are really important and will also help to detoxify the system. Flax oil is best mixed with yogurt. Exercise is also vital for the recovering addict. Sweating will help cleanse the toxins out of the body, and getting the heart rate up and the muscles moving will uplift and heal the ailing body.

ACUPUNCTURE. Acupuncture is being used more and more often with addicts to ward off cravings. Acupuncture is an ancient Chinese method of placing tiny, painless needles in strategic points all over the body. The points correspond to energy meridians, and they restore balance to the body. Ear point acupuncture is often offered in methadone clinics for heroin addicts. In clinics in Oregon, heroin addicts are required to try acupuncture before getting methadone.

MEDITATION. Meditation is focusing intently on one sound, idea, image or goal. For a person recovering from addiction, meditation can be extremely difficult. It can also be extremely valuable. When someone stops to look at waves crashing on the beach or a candle flame or even a tree in the park, often that person will enter into a trance-like state. This is a form of meditation. Artists of all types often become so involved it the act of making art that it becomes a meditation.

Concentration is one of the most difficult tasks for recovering addicts. Thoughts and obsessions run like wildfire through the mind. Meditating is like going on vacation in the mind even while the body is stuck in one spot. Meditation also helps with insomnia (sleeplessness), a problem for many recovering addicts. Meditation before bed (but not in bed) helps to create deep and peaceful sleep.

MANTRAS. A mantra is simply a sound, word, or phrase that is repeated over and over as during meditation. A lot of people think the best mantras are the ones that have no distinct meaning, the ones that are simply sounds. (For instance, the sound "ohm" is a popular choice.) This is so that the meditator will not begin thinking about meditation. The goal of meditation is to go to a place of focus where passing, neurotic thoughts do not interfere with relaxation.

The most important factors in healing from addiction are honesty and love of self. Without those fundamental foundations, no treatment plan can work. Once the addict admits to being sick and needing help, he or she is ready to begin the long road to feeling whole again. The addiction has likely become a great comfort to the addict, something he believes he can't do without. Giving up that idea and letting go of the substance itself is not easy. But it can be done, and it is done every day. The happiness that will come as a

---

HOW TO MEDITATE

The first thing one needs to do is find a safe, quiet space where one will not be disturbed. (Meditation in bed is not recommended.) Sometimes people use a meditation cushion to sit on (this can simply be a pillow or couch cushion). Comfort is essential for meditation. Sitting in a chair, or against the wall if this is more comfortable, is fine, too. Having the feet fall asleep can get in the way of the practice.

Meditation begins by breathing. Breathing should be natural and one should try to be aware of each breath taken. Then the mantra should be repeated, over and over, slowly, in the mind. Obsessive thoughts may creep into the mind during meditation. Meditation teachers suggest that those starting a practice should try to let their thoughts go and use the metaphor of the movie screen. Some people like to pretend that their mind is a movie screen and that the thoughts passing are not their own. This is a good way to detach from painful thoughts. When people try to control their thoughts, or punish themselves for their thoughts, they have a lot of trouble with meditation. Gentle return to the mantra is suggested when thoughts stray. It is important not to get frustrated because thoughts will naturally stray. Twenty minutes per session is usually recommended, but five minutes is good for a starting practice. Healing may not be immediate with meditation, but recovering addicts who have learned to meditate report tremendous benefits from their practice.

result of being free from addiction makes the pain of letting go far more than worth it. Just as getting hooked changed one's life, it will change again, for the better, by kicking the addiction.

COMPULSIVE BEHAVIORS

Compulsions are habitual behaviors or mental acts an individual is driven to perform in order to reduce stress and anxiety. Individuals can fall victim to compulsive behaviors that make them feel a craving similar to that of drug addicts and alcoholics. Just like addiction to drugs and alcohol, this kind of compulsion can affect anyone. Psychological vulnerability, cultural and social factors, and contact with others engaging in compulsive behaviors all play a role in whether an individual will become addicted to a certain ac-

Slot machines are a popular (and often addicting) form of gambling for adults.
(Photograph by Robert J. Huffman. Field Mark Publications. Reproduced by permission.)

tivity. It is important to note that any of the following activities or behaviors in moderation is fine. It is when normal activity begins to affect a person's quality of life that it may be turning compulsive.

Gambling

Gambling can be a dangerous compulsion. Compulsive gamblers often spend all their money, their savings, and even resort to stealing money from loved ones to support their habit. People can get addicted to betting on sports events, playing poker, or playing slot machines in bars and casinos. Something about the possibility of winning, perhaps the risk and the consequent adrenaline rush, spur on the compulsive gambler. Now there is even online gambling. Virtual casinos are immediately available to those who cannot travel to popular gambling destinations like Las Vegas, Nevada, or Atlantic City, New Jersey. The Center for Online Addiction (www.netaddiction.com) exists to serve people with all forms of Internet addiction, including addiction to online gambling. Addiction to online auction houses, such as E-bay, is another form of compulsive gambling. Online traders, people who trade stocks on the Internet, can also fall victim to compulsive trading.

Internet Addiction

Internet addiction is a broad term that describes many kinds of compulsive behaviors. Many of the things that individuals can become addicted to in real life are replicated on the Internet. The reason internet addictions are a bit more dangerous is that people often feel secluded sitting in front of their computer screens. There is a sense that they won't get caught in the act.

Internet addicts can find themselves staring at a computer screen for hours at a time. (Photograph by Robert J. Huffman. Field Mark Publications. Reproduced by permission.)

According the Center for Online Addiction, there are five types of Internet addiction:

- Cyber-sexual addiction is an addiction to adult chat rooms or cyber-porn.
- Cyber-relationship addiction is addiction to meeting people on the Internet, usually in chat rooms or through newsgroups. People who grow addicted to meeting people in the virtual world often stop seeing and speaking to their friends from real life.
- Net compulsions are the gambling-related activities mentioned above.
- Information overload is compulsive web surfing and researching. Sometimes information overload can keep people up all night surfing, which impacts normal daily activities.

- General computer addiction describes those who compulsively play video games or program their computers.

People who hide out in a cyber universe are often troubled and have difficulty socializing with real people. Counseling is suggested to help Internet addicts come out from behind their computers and rejoin the real world.

Exercise Addiction

Exercise addiction is compulsively exercising to the point of damaging a person's health. Is it possible to be addicted to a seemingly healthy behavior? Anything done in excess is dangerous, even if it is taking vitamins or exercising. Individuals addicted to exercise want to do it all the time. They think about exercise constantly, and plan their every moment around the next time they can run, bike, take a class at the gym, or lift weights. They talk constantly about fitness. They begin to associate only with those people who will indulge their addiction: those who also exercise all the time. If someone gets really angry or depressed by missing a workout, or if he or she constantly exercises and stops taking part in other social activities, that individual might be an exercise addict.

Exercise addiction can lead to exhaustion and death. Women can stop getting their periods, and men who are obsessed with muscles sometimes succumb to taking dangerous steroids to bulk up. For most people, a new exercise regimen, often under the supervision of a doctor or a trainer, is truly beneficial to their health. But in some cases, people become so addicted to their regimen that they cannot stop. The healthful benefits of exercise get lost within the desperate need to be exercising all the time.

Often exercise addiction is related to body image disorders, like anorexia nervosa, bulimia nervosa, and body dysmorphic disorder. In all three of these illnesses, the individual sees herself not as she is, but as a distorted, fat person who does not measure up to society's standards of thinness. (In the case of body dysmorphic disorder, fat is not always the culprit but rather a constant unhappiness with parts of or the shape of one's body.) Women and girls tend to suffer from this kind of disease most often, but boys and men are not exempt.

Exercise addiction can develop for other reasons as well. For instance, athletes can become addicted to training in their quest to improve their performance. Abuse of steroids can result from exercise addiction. Steroids are a class of drugs that increase the male hormone testosterone in the body. This increases muscle mass when accompanied by weight training. In the weight lifting world, there is a focus on looking "buff" or very muscular. Many men (women, too) who weight train sometimes become so focused on the goal of attaining huge muscles that they turn to steroids and other artificial means of bulking up.

[See Chapter 12: Mental Illness for more information on body dysmorphic disorder. See Chapter 13: Eating Disorders for more information on exercise addiction and eating disorders.]

Self-Mutilation

Self-mutilation, also known as cutting, is a form of obsessive-compulsive disorder. Self-mutilators tend to be teenage girls, but anyone can have this compulsion. People who self-mutilate often get a high off of seeing their own blood. They sometimes carve on their body with razor blades, stick themselves with pins, and squeeze and pinch their faces. Depression is a common cause for self-mutilation. Many self-mutilators physically hurt themselves to disguise some emotional pain they might be trying to repress. Self-mutilators are not necessarily suicidal, but the fact that they draw blood from their bodies makes outsiders think so. It is important that self-mutilators receive therapy to uncover the reasons why they are hurting themselves.

Manias

A mania is an excessive or unreasonable enthusiasm for something, especially something destructive such as stealing or starting fires.

Kleptomania is the compulsion to steal. Kleptomaniacs lead dangerous lives, stealing things every chance they get. It's not enough for them to simply shoplift from stores. Kleptomaniacs steal from their friends, teachers, and loved ones. Similar to gambling, something about the risk of getting caught gives these individuals a kind of high.

Pyromaniacs are compelled to start fires. This compulsion can kill not just the individual who sets the fire, but anyone caught in the way. Often this compulsion begins in young people who for some reason feel as if they didn't get enough attention as a child. Pyromaniacs are often angry people, but the anger is often suppressed. Setting fires is a way for them to express their anger. Usually pyromaniacs don't get help until it is too late. A serious fire is often what finally gets them into therapy.

Compulsive Shopping

Compulsive shopping is a behavior that was first given media attention in the 1990s. People

Compulsive shoplifting and stealing is called kleptomania. (Photograph © 1999 L. Steinmark. Custom Medical Stock Photo. Reproduced by permission.)

with this addiction run up their credit card bills and get so buried in debt that they sometimes have to declare bankruptcy (legally declared unable to pay one's bills due to lack of money). Many people, at one time or another, purchase an item that they do not really need or want. Compulsive shoppers, however, will go on frequent shopping sprees and buy many things that they just don't need at all. Somehow, standing in front of the item before they buy it, they believe that their lives will be better if they own the item. As a result, they end up with closets full of unnecessary items.

Compulsive shoppers are searching for love in the form of material objects. They think that things will provide them with the emotional lack in their lives. Often they will continue going on shopping binges until a loved one stops them or they lose everything to debt. A self-motivated method for stopping compulsive shopping is putting credit cards into a block of ice in the freezer. Then the individual desiring to shop will have to wait until the ice melts to retrieve the card, and hopefully the compulsion will have passed by that time. Professional help is suggested for those individuals who cannot control shopping binges.

Sex Addiction

Sex addiction is the compulsion to repeatedly seek out people and have sexual intercourse with them. Sex addicts put themselves in dangerous situations regularly just to fulfil their need to have sex with someone. People who are sex addicts sometimes meet strangers in bars, or almost anywhere, and go someplace with that stranger to engage in casual sexual activity. Of course, when a stranger is involved there is a great deal of danger from potential personal harm. People who engage in such behaviors are not just being promiscuous; rather, they are psychologically driven to their sex addiction.

Sex addiction is treatable. Once addicts confront and accept their behavior, they can begin to look at the reasons why they are compelled to have sex all the time. Often sex addicts experienced sexual abuse as children. Their sex addiction is a way of having control over their bodies and the act of seduction they compulsively perform is a way of having control over a partner. Sex addiction is never connected to healthy love and desire.

A strong self-image is the first defense against any type of addiction. Many of the habits and behaviors discussed in this chapter are not alarming if imagined in small doses. A cup of coffee, a candy bar, running for good health, or sexual activity isn't dangerous if it is treated as a simple desire that can be fulfilled and then forgotten about. (However, the mind-altering drugs and alcohol discussed in this chapter can be dangerous, even if they are just experimented with even one time.) It is most important to remember that if one has a strong sense of self and a strong support system, addiction is far less likely to result from experimentation.

Books

Fields, Richard. *Drugs in Perspective.* New York: McGraw Hill, 1998.

Periodicals

Peele, Stanton. "The Cure for Adolescent Drug Abuse: Worse Than the Problem?" *Journal of Counseling and Development.* 65: 23-24, 1986.

Web sites

Addiction Research Foundation. [Online] http://www.arf.org (Accessed July 10, 1999).

Al-Anon and Alateen. [Online] http://www.Al-Anon-Alateen.org/ (Accessed July 10, 1999).

Campaign for Tobacco-Free Kids—Kids' Corner. [Online] http://www.tobaccofreekids.org/html/kids__corner.html (Accessed July 10, 1999).

The Center For Online Addiction. [Online] http://www.netaddiction.com/net_compulsions.htm (Accessed June 30, 1999).

D.A.R.E. Kids. [Online] http://www.dare-america.com/index2.htm (Accessed June 30, 1999).

Facts for Families. [Online] http://www.aacap.org/web/aacap/FactsFam/teendrug.htm (Accessed July 10, 1999).

Heath, Mary. *The Benefits of Zen Meditation in Addiction and Recovery.* [Online] http://www.viacorp.com/addiction.html/ (Accessed July 10, 1999).

NCADI for Kids Only. [Online] http://www.health.org/kidsarea/index.htm (Accessed July 10, 1999).

The School Zone. [Online] http://www.theschoolzone.org/ (Accessed July 10, 1999).

Smoke-Free Kids. [Online] http://www.smokefree.gov/ (Accessed July 10, 1999).

Teen Challenge World Wide Network. [Online] http://www.teenchallenge.com (Accessed July 10, 1999).

Teen Voices. [Online] http://www.teenvoices.com/ (Accessed June 30, 1999).

Tips 4 Kids—CDC's Tobacco Info-Youth Page. [Online] http://www.cdc.gov/nccdphp/osh/tipskids.htm (Accessed July 10, 1999).

15

Mental Health Therapies

What usually comes to mind when one hears the words "mental illness" or "mental health"? Many people might think of the stereotypical images of "crazy people" or of mental institutions. While this may be the case for many afflicted with mental illness, huge advancements have been made in the field of mental health therapies.

Today, many people who suffer from some form of mental illness can enjoy relatively normal lives with the help of certain therapy treatments and other aids. Strides in different branches of mental health therapies as well as considerable advances in drug therapy have contributed to the effectiveness of psychology (the scientific study of mental processes and behaviors) and psychiatry (the branch of medicine that relates to the study and treatment of mental illness).

There is no easy answer as to what kind of therapy might be the best for someone who is in need. The choice will vary from person to person since each person and his or her mental illness is different. Talking to one's doctor or another trustworthy adult and conducting a little research are good ways to gain the knowledge needed to make the right choices regarding therapy's road to recovery.

Psychotherapy

Insight Therapy

Cognitive and Behavior Therapies

Nontraditional Mental Health Therapy Techniques

Therapy Formats

Self-Help

PSYCHOTHERAPY

Psychotherapy is, like many aspects in the field of mental health, a theory, but it is one widely believed and accepted worldwide. Psychotherapy is the general term for an interaction in which a trained professional, usually a therapist or analyst, tries to help a patient by following a certain psychological theory or school of thought, to address problems based on emotional suffering, behavioral problems, or a disorder. Through a bond of trust that is developed between therapist and patient, the patient can achieve goals in therapy, such as the elimination of negative behavior and an improvement in well-being.

The numerous mental health therapy techniques and therapies available today are used to tackle a wide variety of conditions such as depression, anxiety disorders, eating disorders, and phobias, as well as borderline disorders, multiple personality disorder, and schizophrenia. These conditions can be treated, often successfully, with the help of psychotherapy and, sometimes, supplementary drug therapy.

Today, therapists are becoming more and more concerned with finding the most appropriate form of therapy for an individual. There are numerous mental health techniques available, and their effectiveness varies from patient to patient. A positive therapy experience, where success is gained, must comprise a constructive relationship between therapist and patient. Often, a patient's problems cannot be trimmed to fit into one category; sometimes an individual's problems overlap as a result of years of unaddressed and accumulated inner and outer conflict. In these cases the treatment becomes more complicated. The key, however, starts with a good match between an informed, understanding, sensitive therapist and the patient.

WORDS TO KNOW

Art therapy: The use of art forms and craft activities to treat emotional, mental and physical disabilities.

Bioenergetics: Body/mind therapy that stresses the body and the mind being freed of negative actions.

Biofeedback: The technique of making unconscious or involuntary bodily processes (as heartbeats or brain waves) perceptible in order to manipulate them by conscious mental control.

Classic conditioning: Learning involving automatic response to a certain stimulus that is acquired and reinforced through association.

Cognition: The grouping of the mental processes of perception, recognition, conception, judgment, and reason.

Dance therapy: The use of dance and movement to treat or alleviate symptoms associated with mental or physical illness.

Dream analysis: A technique of Freudian therapy that involves looking closely at a patient's dreams for symbolism and significance of themes and/or repressed thoughts.

Ego: The part of one's personality that balances the drives of the id and the exterior world that is the center of the superego.

Existential therapy: Therapy that stresses the importance of existence and urges patients to take responsibility for their psychological existence and well-being.

Gestalt therapy: A humanistic therapy that urges individuals to satisfy growing needs, acknowledge previously unexpressed feelings, and reclaim facets of their personalities that have been denied.

Humanistic: A philosophy that places importance on human interests and dignity, stressing the individual over the religious or spiritual.

Hypnosis: A trance-like state of consciousness brought about by suggestions of relaxation, which is marked by increased suggestibility.

Id: According to Sigmund Freud, the biological instincts that revolve around pleasure, especially sexual and aggressive impulses.

INSIGHT THERAPY

Insight therapy is the umbrella term used to describe a group of different therapy techniques that have some similar characteristics in theory and thought. Insight therapy assumes that a person's behavior, thoughts, and emotions become disordered because the individual does not understand what motivates him, especially when a conflict develops between the person's needs and his drives. The theory of insight therapy, therefore, is that a greater awareness of motivation will result in an increase in control and an improvement in thought, emotion, and behavior. The goal of this therapy is to help an individual discover the reasons and motivation for his behavior, feelings, and thinking. The different types of insight therapies are described below.

Psychoanalysis

Labeled by some as the "Father of Psychoanalysis," Sigmund Freud (1856–1939) laid the groundwork for many forms of mental health therapies with his introduction of psychoanalysis and the psychoanalytic or psychodynamic paradigm, which states that psychopathology (the study of the

Insight therapy: A group of different therapy techniques that assume that a person's behavior, thoughts, and emotions become disordered as a result of the individual's lack of understanding as to what motivates him or her.

Modeling: Learning based on modeling one's behavior on that of another person with whom an individual strongly identifies.

Music therapy: The use of music to treat or alleviate symptoms associated with certain mental or physical illnesses.

Operant conditioning: Learning involving voluntary response to a certain stimuli based on positive or negative consequences resulting from the response.

Pharmacotherapy: The use of medication to treat emotional and mental problems.

Psychiatry: The branch of medicine that relates to the study and treatment of mental illness.

Psychoanalysis: A theory of psychotherapy, based on the work of Sigmund Freud, involving dream analysis, free association, and different facets of the self (id, ego, superego).

Psychodrama: A therapy that involves a patient enacting or reenacting life situations in order to gain insight and alter behavior. The patient is the actor while the therapist is the director.

Psychodynamics: The forces (emotional and mental) that develop in early childhood and how they affect behavior and mental well-being.

Psychology: The scientific study of mental processes and behaviors.

Psychotherapy: The general term of an interaction in which a trained mental health professional tries to help a patient resolve emotional and mental distress.

Rational-emotive behavior therapy: Therapy that seeks to identify a patient's irrational beliefs as the key to changing behavior rather than examining the cause of the conflict itself.

Reality therapy: A therapy that empowers people to make choices and control their destinies.

Superego: According to Sigmund Freud, the part of one's personality that is concerned with social values and rules.

nature and development of mental disorders) is a result of "unconscious conflicts" within a person.

Freud believed that personal development is based on inborn, and particularly sexual, drives that exist in everyone. He also believed that the mind, which he renamed the psyche, is divided into three parts. Functioning together as a whole, these three parts represent specific energies in a person.

THE ID. Present at birth, the id is the part of the mind in charge of all the energy needed to "run" the psyche. It comprises the basic biological urges for food, water, elimination, warmth, affection, and sex. (Originally trained as a neurologist, Freud believed that the source of all of the id's energy is biological.) Later, as a child develops, the energy from the psyche, or the libido, is converted into unconscious psychic energy. The id works on immediate gratification and operates on what Freud called the pleasure principle: A primary process, the id strives to rid the psyche of developing tension by utilizing the pleasure principle, which is the tendency to avoid or reduce pain and obtain pleasure. A classic example describes an infant who, when hungry, works under the pleasure principle to overcome his discomfort when he reaches for his mother's breast.

THE EGO. A primarily conscious part of the psyche, the ego develops during the second half of an infant's first year, and deals with reality and the conscious situations surrounding an individual. Through planning and decision making, which is also called secondary process thinking, the ego learns that operating on the id level is generally not very effective in the long term. The ego, then, operates through realistic thinking, or on the reality principle. The ego gets its energy from the id, which it is also in charge of directing.

Sigmund Freud. (The Library of Congress.)

THE SUPEREGO. The superego, which develops throughout childhood, operates more or less as a person's conscience. According to Freud, the superego is the part of the mind that houses the rules of the society in which one lives (the conscience), a person's goals, and how one wants to behave (called the ego-ideal). While the id and ego are considered characteristics of the individual, the superego is based more on outside influences, such as family and society. For example, as children grow up, they will learn what actions and behaviors are or are not acceptable; from this new knowledge, they learn how to act to win the praise or affection of a parent.

Freud believed that the superego develops from the ego much as the ego develops from the id. Both the id's instincts and many superego activities are unknown to the mind, while the ego is always conscious of all the psyche's activities. These three parts of the psyche work together in a relationship called psychodynamics.

Psychoanalytic theory and psychoanalysis are based on Freud's second theory of neurotic anxiety, which is the reaction of the ego when a previously repressed id impulse pushes to express itself. The unconscious part of the ego, for example, encounters a situation that reminds it of a repressed childhood conflict, often related to a sexual or aggressive impulse, and is overcome by an overwhelming feeling of tension. Psychoanalytic therapy tries to remove the earlier repression and helps the patient resolve the childhood conflict through the use of adult reality. The childhood repression had prevented the ego from growing; as the conflict is faced and resolved, the ego can reenter a healthy growth pattern.

FREE ASSOCIATION. Raising repressed conflicts occurs through different psychoanalytic techniques, one of which is called free association. In free association, the patient reclines on a couch, facing away from the analyst. The analyst sits near the patient's head and will often take notes during a session. The patient is then free to talk without censoring of any kind. Eventually defenses held by the patient should lessen, and a bond of trust between analyst and patient is established.

DREAM ANALYSIS. Another analytic technique often used in psychoanalysis is dream analysis. This technique follows the Freudian theory that ego defenses are relaxed during sleep, which allows repressed material to enter the sleeper's consciousness. Since these repressed thoughts are so threatening they cannot be experienced in their actual form; the thoughts are disguised in dreams. The dreams, then, become symbolic and significant to the patient's psychoanalytic work.

TRANSFERENCE. Yet another ingredient in psychoanalysis is transference, a patient's response to the analyst which is not in keeping with the analyst-patient relationship but seems, instead, to resemble ways of behaving toward significant people in the patient's past. For example, as a result of feeling neglected as children, patients may feel that they must impress the analyst in order to keep the analyst present. Through observation of these transferred attitudes, the analyst gains insight into the childhood origin of repressed conflicts. The analyst might find that patients who were often home alone as children due to the hardworking but unaware parents could only gain the parental attention they craved when they acted in extreme ways.

One focus of psychoanalysis is the analysis of defenses. This can provide the analyst with a clearer picture of some of the patient's conflict. The therapist studies the patient's defense mechanisms, which are the ego's uncon-

To establish trust between a patient and her analyst, psychoanalytic sessions may occur as frequently as five times a week at the beginning of a relationship. (Photograph © 1994 Peter Berndt. Custom Medical Stock Photo. Reproduced by permission.)

scious way of warding off a confrontation with anxiety. An example of a defense mechanism would occur when a person who does not want to discuss the death of a close friend or relative during her session might experience a memory lapse when the topic is introduced and she is forced to discuss it. The analyst tries to interpret this patient's behavior, pointing out its defensive nature in order to stimulate the patient to realize that she is avoiding the topic.

Psychoanalytic sessions between patients and their analysts may occur as frequently as five times a week. This frequency is necessary at the beginning of the relationship in order to establish trust between patient and analyst and therefore bring the patient to a level of comfort where repressed conflicts can be uncovered and discussed.

Humanistic and Existential Therapies

Humanistic and existential therapies are therapy techniques that also fall under the category of insight therapies. These therapies are insight-focused, that is, they are based on the assumption that disordered behavior can be overcome by increasing patients' own awareness of their motivations and needs. Whereas psychoanalysis assumes that human nature (the id) is something in need of restraint, humanistic and existential therapists place more emphasis on a person's freedom of choice. Humanistic and existential therapists believe that free will is a person's most valuable trait and is considered a gift to be used wisely. Existential theorists agreed with Freud on some counts, but disagreed on others, which led many to branch out and develop their own therapy techniques.

ANALYTICAL PSYCHOLOGY. Carl Gustav Jung (1887–1961) was one of the theorists who decided to branch out on his own. He defined analytical psychology, which is a mixture of Freudian and humanistic psychology. Jung believed that the role of the unconscious was very important in human behavior. In addition to our unconscious, Jung said there is a collective unconscious as well, which acts as a storage area for all the experiences that all people have had over the centuries; it also, he said, contains positive and creative forces rather than sexual and aggressive ones, as Freud argued. Carl Jung believed that we all have masculine and feminine traits that can be blended within a person; he also thought our spiritual and religious needs are just as important as our libidinal, or physical, sexual needs.

Analytical psychology organizes personality types into groups; the familiar terms "extroverted," or acting out, and "introverted," or turning oneself inward, are Jungian terms used to describe personality traits. Developing a purpose, decision-making, and setting goals are other components of Jung's theory. Whereas Freud believed that a person's current and future behavior is based on experiences of the past, Jungian theorists often focus on dreams, fantasies, and other things that come from or involve the unconscious. Jungian therapy, then, focuses on an analysis of the patient's unconscious processes so the patient can ultimately integrate them into conscious thought and deal with them. Much of the Jungian technique is based on bringing the unconscious into the conscious.

In explaining personality, Jung said there are three levels of consciousness: the conscious, the personal unconscious, and the collective unconscious.

The conscious is the only level of which a person is directly aware. This awareness begins right at birth and continues throughout a person's life. At one point, the conscious experiences a stage called individuation, in which the person strives to be different from others and assert him-

PSYCHODYNAMIC THERAPY

In 1946, psychodynamic therapy was developed in part through the work of Franz Gabriel Alexander, M.D., and Thomas Morton French, M.D., who were supporters of a briefer analytic therapy than Freud's psychoanalytic theory, using a present and more future-oriented approach. Influenced by such Freudian concepts as the defense mechanism and unconscious motivation, psychodynamic therapy is more active than Freudian therapy and focuses more on present problems and relationships than on childhood conflicts. A briefer, less intensive therapy form, the session frequency and the patient's body position in this therapy matter less than what the patient says and does. With support from the therapist, patients in psychodynamic therapy slowly examine the true sources of their tension and unhappiness by facing repressed feelings and eventually lifting that repression.

self as an individual. The goal of individuation is to know oneself wholly and completely. This is accomplished, in part, by bringing unconscious material to the conscious.

The personal unconscious is the landing area of the brain for the thoughts, feelings, experiences, and perceptions that are not picked up by the ego. Repressed personal conflicts or unresolved issues are also stored here. Jung wove this concept into his psychoanalytic theory: often thoughts, memories and other material in the personal unconscious are associated with each other and form an involuntary theme. Jung assigned the term "complex" to describe this theme. These complexes can have an extreme emotional effect on a person.

The idea of the collective unconscious is one that separates Jung's theory of psychotherapy from other theories. Jung said the collective unconscious is made up of images and ideas that are independent of the material in one's personal consciousness. Also present in the collective unconscious are instincts, or strong motivations that are present from birth, and archetypes, which are universally known images or symbols that predispose an individual to have a specific feeling or thought about that image. Archetypes will often show themselves in the form of archetypal images, such as the archetype of death or the archetype of the old woman; death's definition is pretty clear (death equals death) and the archetype of the old woman is often used as a representation of wisdom and age.

Jung believed that to fully understand people, one has to appreciate a person's dreams and not just his or her past experiences. Through analytical psychology, the therapist and patient work together to uncover both parts of the person and address conflicts existing in that person.

ADLERIAN PSYCHOLOGY. After a childhood full of traumatic events and serious illness, Alfred Adler (1870–1937) first experienced an interest in psychology while working as a general medical practitioner. After working in this position for a few years, Adler realized he wanted to learn about his patients' social and psychological situations, so he became a psychiatrist (a medical doctor who specializes in the area of the mind). This interest in the whole person was to affect his future work for years to come.

Although at first a member of Freud's psychoanalytic circle, Adler soon branched out on his own and found an interest in the study of the subjectivity of perception as well as the importance of social factors on an individual, as opposed to the importance of biological factors asserted by Freud. Adler's view of personality stressed the importance of the person as a whole but also of the individual's interaction with surrounding society. He also saw the person as a goal-directed, creative individual responsible for his own future.

Because he had been quite ill as a child, Adler had to overcome his own feelings of extreme inferiority (feeling less worthy than others) throughout his childhood. As a result, he emphasized in his own theories of working toward superiority, but not in an antisocial sense. Instead, he viewed people as tied to their surroundings; Adler claimed that a person's fulfillment was based on doing things for the "social good." Like Jung, Adler also argued the importance of working toward personal goals in therapy.

The main factor in Adler's work was a focus on individual psychology, or individual phenomenology—working to help patients get over the "illogical expectations" made on themselves and their lives. He believed that to feel better one must increase one's focus on rational thinking. This belief followed the Jungian theory that the goal of one's life should be individuation, or the conscious realization of one's psychological reality—a reality unlike any other, unique to only that person. As patients become more and more aware of themselves, they combine the unconscious and conscious parts of themselves, thereby becoming stronger and more emotionally whole.

Believing that a person's growth was based on relationships with family during the early years of development, Adler's interest in psychological growth, the prevention of problems, and the improvement of society influenced the creation of child development centers and parent education.

TECHNIQUES AND GOALS OF ADLERIAN THERAPY. Crucial to the Adlerian therapy technique is the establishment of a good therapeutic relationship between therapist and patient, particularly one based on respect and mutual trust. In order for this to happen, therapists and patients must share the same goals for their relationships, which are often uncovered to patients by the therapists. This often includes encouragement by the therapists that the patients can indeed reach their goals through working together with their therapists.

Therapists may also introduce to patients any signs of self-abusive behaviors on the part of the patients, such as resisting or missing therapy sessions. Above all, Adlerian therapists are supportive and empathetic (understanding) to patients; as patients gradually discuss more and more with their therapists, the Adlerians develop knowledge of the lifestyles of their patients. Empathetic responses on the therapists' part often reflect a developed understanding of patients' lifestyles. One of the most important goals of Adlerian therapy is the patient's increase in social interests, as well as an increase in self-awareness and self-confidence.

Adlerian therapy is a practical, humanistic therapy method that helps individuals to identify and change the dysfunction in their lives.

Existential therapy

Another insight therapy, existential therapy is based on the philosophical theory of existentialism, which emphasizes the importance of existence, including one's responsibility for one's own psychological existence. One important component of this theory is dealing with life themes instead of techniques; more than other therapies, existential therapy looks at a patient's self-awareness and his ability to look beyond the immediate problems and events in his or her life and focus instead on problems of human existence.

The first existential therapists were trained in Freud's theories of psychoanalysis, but they disagreed with Freud's stress on the importance of biological drives and unconscious processes in the psyche. Instead, these therapists saw their patients as they were in reality, not as subjects based on theory.

The concepts of existential therapy developed out of the writings of European philosophers, such as Soren Kierkegaard, Friedrich Nietzsche, Karl Jaspers, philosopher and theologian Martin Heidegger, and the writer and philosopher Jean-Paul Sartre.

TECHNIQUES AND GOALS OF EXISTENTIAL THERAPY. With existential therapy, the focus is not on technique but on existential themes and how they apply to the patient. Through a positive, constructive therapeutic relationship between therapist and patient, existential therapy uncovers common themes occurring in the patient's life. Patients discover that they are not living their lives to the full potential and learn what they must do to realize their full capacity.

The existential therapist must be fully aware of patients and their needs in order to help them attain that position of living to the full of their existence. As patients become more aware of themselves and the results of their actions, they take more responsibility for life and become more "active."

Person-centered Therapy

Once called nondirective therapy, then client-centered therapy, person-centered therapy was developed by American psychologist Carl Rogers. Drawing from years of in-depth clinical research, Rogers's therapy is based on four stages: the developmental stage, the nondirective stage, the client-centered stage, and the person-centered stage.

Person-centered therapy looks at assumptions made about human nature and how people can try to understand these assumptions. Like other humanistic therapists, Rogers believed that people should be responsible for themselves, even when they are troubled. Person-centered therapy takes a positive view of patients, believing that they tend to move toward being fully functioning instead of wallowing in their problems.

TECHNIQUES AND GOALS OF PERSON-CENTERED THERAPY. Person-centered therapy is based more on a way of being rather than a therapy technique. Focusing on understanding and caring instead of diagnosis and advice, Rogers believed that change in the patient could take place if only a few criteria were met: 1. The patient must be anxious or incongruent (lacking harmony) and be in contact with the therapist. 2. The therapist must be genuine; that is, a therapist's words and feelings must agree. 3. The therapist must accept the client and care unconditionally for the client. In addition, the therapist must understand the patient's thoughts and experiences and relay this understanding to the patient.

Rogerian therapists follow the nondirective approach. Although they may want to aid the patient in making decisions that may prove difficult for the patient to realize alone, the therapist cannot provide the answers because a patient must come to conclusions alone. The therapist does not ask questions in a person-centered therapy session, as they may hamper the patient's personal growth, the goal of this therapy.

If the patient is able to perceive these conditions offered by the therapist, then the therapeutic change in the patient will take place and personal growth and higher consciousness can be reached.

Gestalt Therapy

Gestalt psychology rose from the work of Frederich S. Perls, who felt that a focus on perception, and on the development of the whole individual, were important. This was attained by increasing the patient's awareness of unacknowledged feelings and becoming aware of parts of the patient's personality that had been previously denied.

Gestalt therapy has both humanistic and existential aspects; Perls's contemporaries primarily rejected it because Perls disagreed with some of the basic concepts of psychoanalytic theory, such as the importance of the libido and its various transformations in the development of neurosis (mental disorders). Originally developed in the 1940s, the overall concepts of the Gestalt theory state that people are basically good and that this goodness should be allowed to show itself; also, psychological problems originate in frustrations and denials of this innate goodness.

TECHNIQUES AND GOALS OF GESTALT THERAPY. Gestalt therapists focus on the creative aspects of people, instead of their problematic parts. There is a focus on the patient in the therapy room, in the present, instead of a launching into the past; what is most important for the patient is what is happening in that room at that time. If the past enters a session and creates problems for the Gestalt patient, it is brought into the present and discussed. The question of "why" is discouraged in Gestalt therapy, because trying to find causes in the past is considered an attempt to escape the responsibility for decisions made in the present. The therapist plays a role, too: Patients are sometimes coerced (forced) or even bullied into an awareness of every minute detail of the present situation.

Perls believed that awareness acted as a curative, so it is an integral part of this therapy process. He created quite a few techniques for patients, but one well-known practice is the empty chair technique, where a patient projects and then faces those projections. When a patient projects, the ego rejects characteristics or thoughts that are unacceptable or difficult to focus on consciously. For example, a patient may have unresolved feelings about a parent's early death. The patient in Gestalt therapy will sit facing an empty chair and pretend that he is facing the dead parent. The patient can then consciously face, and eventually overcome, the unresolved feelings or conflicts toward that parent.

The goal of Gestalt therapy is to help patients understand and accept their needs and fears as well as increase awareness of how they keep themselves from reaching their goals and taking care of their needs. Also, the Gestalt therapist strives to help the patient encounter the world in a nonjudgmental way. Concentration on the "here and now" and on the patient as responsible for his or her actions and behavior is an end result.

COGNITIVE AND BEHAVIOR THERAPIES

Cognition is the term used for the grouping of the mental processes of perceiving, recognizing, conceiving, judging, and reasoning. Cognition is based on how not just humans but all living creatures adjust their experiences, how they make sense of these experiences, and how they relate present experiences to past ones embedded in memory. This is called the cognitive paradigm and is commonly accepted by psychologists. Cognitive theory is based on the idea that the learning process is very complex and one's belief system and ways of thinking are very important when it comes to determining and affecting behavior and feelings.

Psychoanalyst Aaron Beck (1921–) developed cognitive therapy. Beck was intrigued by how people spoke to themselves through their own self-communication system. When his patients experienced thoughts that they were hardly aware of and these thoughts did not seem to stem from the free association technique practiced in sessions, Beck stressed that the patient focus on these thoughts, which he renamed automatic thoughts. These unformed thoughts were often connected to unpleasant feelings or memories within the patient.

Through the isolation of and focus on these unformed thoughts, Beck was able to identify negative themes that characterized the way patients considered both present and past situations. From these unformed thoughts, patients formed rules for themselves, which Beck called schemas. These schemas, especially within depressed people, were self-defeating and often leaned toward the negative.

Techniques and Goals of Cognitive Therapy

Like Alfred Adler, Aaron Beck believes in an active approach to therapy, including the use of direct dialogue with the patient. Another significant approach to cognitive therapy is based on the ideas of cognitive therapist Albert Ellis, who asserted that negative feelings and activities are caused by irrational beliefs within a person. For example, a child may believe that in order to win the love of his parents he must be a "perfect" son. This, of course, is an irrational thought—no one can be absolutely perfect.

Through a technique called rational-emotive therapy, Ellis and other cognitive therapists who follow his beliefs guide their patients in challenging their irrational beliefs and assist them in replacing such thoughts with new, more positive ones. In the case of the "perfect" son, a cognitive therapist would help him see that although it would be great if he could be perfect, he doesn't have to be without fault to win the love of his parents.

Cognitive therapists see the patient as active in the situation, with the patient's past knowledge imposing a "perceptual funnel" on his experience. The patient is guided into fitting new information into an organized network of already accumulated knowledge, called schema. New life information may fit the schema; if not, the patient reorganizes the new information to fit the schema. In this way, conflicts and issues are unearthed, discussed, and conquered.

Behavior Therapy

The idea of behaviorism was developed primarily by American psychologist John B. Watson, who said that psychology was the study of observable behavior instead of an examination of the patient's subjective experiences. Behaviorism focuses on the study of this observable behavior instead of on consciousness. This is a switch in previous focus from learning to thinking.

Behavior therapy has its history in the experimental psychology and learning processes of humans and animals. Its main focus is to change certain behaviors instead of uncovering unconscious conflicts or problems. The learning/behavioral paradigm states that abnormal behavior is made up of responses learned the same way that normal behavior is learned. Through behaviorism, therapists use ways of learning as part of their technique in helping a patient.

CLASSIC CONDITIONING. Classic conditioning, also called respondent conditioning, was actually discovered by accident by Russian physiologist Ivan Pavlov (1849–1936). One day, while studying the digestive system of his subject (a dog), Pavlov realized that when a bell was rung right before feeding the dog, the dog would salivate before the food was even brought out. The food, then, becomes an unconditioned stimulus (UCS), and the dog's response, salivating, is an unconditioned response (UCR). When the food is preceded by a neutral stimulus, or the ringing of a bell, the sound of the bell, called the conditioned stimulus, or CS, makes the dog salivate, which is the conditioned response (CR).

Extinction is another aspect of this classic conditioning; it refers to what happens to the CR when the repeated sound of the bell is not followed by the food. From this, the dog salivates fewer and fewer times until the CR eventually disappears.

There seems to be no limit, then, to the wide array of stimuli that could be introduced to subjects and followed with the study of different conditioned responses. The study of classical conditioning showed psychologists that there might be a relationship between classical conditioning and the development of emotional disorders.

OPERANT CONDITIONING. Whereas classical conditioning focuses on the introduction of a conditioned stimulus on the subject before introducing an unconditioned stimulus, operant conditioning focuses on the background and results of behavior. The operant theory, based on the work of E.L. Thorndike (1874–1949) and B.F. Skinner (1904–1990), actually formed the roots of much of behavior therapy today.

Operant conditioning is a type of learning based on the effects of consequences on behavior, where one's behavior is changed by systematically changing the surrounding circumstances. Through study, Thorndike developed a principle called the law of effect, which says that behavior followed by consequences that are satisfying to the subject will be repeated, and that behavior followed by negative consequences will be discouraged.

B. F. Skinner. (The Library of Congress.)

Skinner introduced the concept of operant conditioning. He adjusted Thorndike's law of effect by shifting the focus from the linking of stimuli and responses to the relationships between those responses and their consequences. He also introduced the concept of a discriminative stimulus, or an external event that tells an organism that if it performs a certain behavior, a certain consequence will occur.

A classic example of operant conditioning involves the Skinner box, wherein a subject, often a small animal such as a pigeon, is placed into a closed box with a box of lighted knobs. The psychologist will record the number of the subject's pecks at each light according to what each lighted knob corresponds; for example, if the pigeon has been deprived of water, it will peck at the knob corresponding to water more times than it pecks at the other knobs. The subject can even be trained to peck at specific colored lights by reinforcing one knob over another.

Operant conditioning, like classical conditioning, is useful in behavior therapy's study of emotional disorders or abnormalities, but is also helpful in the study of conduct disorder, autism (see Chapter 12: Mental Illness), and children and their behaviors as they age (the concept of a child's "time out"—where a child is sent to his room or asked to sit quietly after misbehaving—for example, is an operant tool).

MODELING. Modeling, another behavior therapy tool, is the learning of a behavior by observing and imitating it. This is especially apparent in children, who learn a significant amount through modeling. Modeling is also a very effective treatment for severely disturbed patients, such as schizophrenics (see Chapter 12: Mental Illness), because it teaches them new social behavior that can improve their functioning in the outer world.

Modeling utilizes cognitive behaviors (perception, reasoning, etc.) to effectively absorb the modeled behavior. Modeling has developed and has been effectively used as a form of cognitive behavior therapy because it provides the subject with a "code" or plan in which to learn the new behavior. Researchers have learned that when subjects have a model or plan to follow, the new information is better retained. Also, the use of this code or plan helps subjects to pattern their own actions on what they have seen modeled. What was at first seen as a simple form of learning has been realized as an effective form of cognitive behavior therapy.

Cognitive Behavior Therapy

Cognitive behavior therapy is just one mode of therapy that falls under the larger umbrella of cognitive and behavior therapies. Cognitive behavior therapy combines pieces of cognitive therapy, which aims to change a person's thinking to affect a change in behavior, and pieces of behavior therapy, which aims to change a person's behavior. Cognitive restructuring is a term utilized by therapists to define a changing thought pattern that is thought to cause an emotional disturbance. This restructuring is administered in many ways by cognitive behavior therapists.

Rational-Emotive Behavior Therapy

The basis of rational-emotive behavior therapy comes from cognitive behavior therapist Albert Ellis, who believed that antisocial, negative feelings and activity are caused by irrational beliefs based on a code one makes for oneself about how to live. Mistakenly, people put extreme demands on themselves and those around them, as when a person who strives to be perfect makes a mistake and feels overwhelmingly terrible; the person will use that internal communication system to punish himself. In addition, people will occasionally attempt to decipher what occurs around them, and these discoveries sometimes cause conflict. Ellis stressed the importance of the therapist's attention on the patient's beliefs instead of what is causing the conflict.

Those who practice rational-emotive behavior therapy differ in the ways in which they persuade patients to adopt new ways of communicating with oneself. Some therapists have been known to tease, coerce, or bully their patients into realizing new forms of self-communication. Others take a different approach and suggest that patients discuss their irrational beliefs and then gently guide them toward a more rational way of living. With this behavior therapy technique, Ellis and his supporters helped their patients rethink their original, negative beliefs and guided them into restructuring those thoughts or beliefs. For example, the man who made the mistake is coached into rethinking the scenario and inserts a realistic thought: although it would be nice to be perfect, everybody makes mistakes at some point.

Rational-emotive behavior therapy (REBT) is a relatively young technique in the field of mental health therapy, and studies about it are still being conducted. The technique has been shown to reduce anxiety and to help patients gain control of some forms of excessive anger and depression, but it has also worked as a preventive tool for untroubled people to help them deal with everyday stress. It has also been used experimentally in classrooms to delay and possibly reduce the amount of emotional problems later in life.

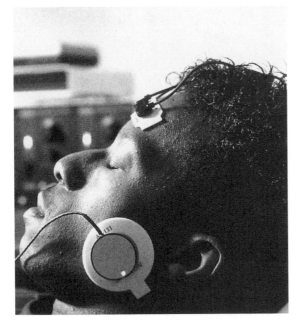

A patient being monitored for stress via biofeedback. (Photograph by Will & Deni McIntyre. Photo Researchers, Inc. Reproduced by permission.)

Behavioral Medicine

Behavioral medicine, also called health psychology, is another developing mental health therapy technique in the field of medicine. It is the interdisciplinary study of ideas and knowledge taken from medicine and behavior science (psychology). It is called interdisciplinary because it incorporates the knowledge of many different medical practitioners, from social workers to psychiatrists and researchers. It is used to understand physical and mental illness as well as to prevent and treat psychophysiological disorders, or physical maladies caused by emotional distress, such as stress and other illnesses that involve the psyche. Behavioral medicine has also been used to study and treat acute and chronic pain.

BIOFEEDBACK. One of the first behavioral medicine techniques finding great success is biofeedback, which uses extremely sensitive machines to provide patients with information on their blood pressure, skin temperature, brain waves, and other bodily functions. The patient, painlessly hooked up to these machines, is given an auditory or visual sign when there is a change in the patient's condition. Learning the signal before one's blood pressure raises, for example, can lead a patient to train himself to identify what behaviors or situations might be causing his raise in blood pressure. The patient, then, can eventually teach himself to control his blood pressure if he has learned from biofeedback to recognize when a raise might occur.

Biofeedback can be a very effective way to combat other stress-induced conditions, such as anxiety, hives, and tension headaches, but it has also proven helpful for patients with attention-deficit disorder (ADD), depression, and other "minor" emotional disturbances (see Chapter 13: Mental Illness).

PAIN MANAGEMENT. The adapting of pain into one's life does not seem like something one would want to learn at all, but for many people pain is a part of every day. Dealing with that maladaptive pain (pain that does not fit with one's situation and seriously limits one's enjoyment of life) without its taking over can be difficult. Researchers have learned that if patients are distracted from their pain, the pain may be lessened when it occurs or may not even be felt at all. Cognitive psychologists have also found that, since everyone has a limited amount of attention to channel toward one stimulus, distracting the patient away from the pain and toward something else guides the patient into focusing all attention on the other stimulus. This human limitation can actually prove beneficial to the sufferer of pain.

REALITY THERAPY

Based on the control theory, which states that people are responsible for their lives and actions, reality therapy was established to help people make choices, both simple and difficult, and ultimately control their behavior.

Psychiatrist William Glasser (1925–), who developed this form of therapy, was not satisfied with psychoanalysis' belief that patients should deny responsibility for their behavior and instead blame others and their past for their problems. Glasser stresses that the relationship between therapist and patient should be friendly, open, and accepting. As the patient commits to therapy and what it uncovers, Glasser believes he can guide the patient toward altering his ways of thinking and feeling.

In reality therapy, talking about one's feelings is accepted, but is not a major focus of the therapy. Instead, Glasser stresses helping clients make changes in their lives and maintaining those changes. The therapist, according to Glasser, should not accept excuses on the patient's part, as this would hinder the healing process.

This therapy technique has attracted interest with professionals in many fields, including therapists, school counselors, substance abuse counselors, and corrections employees. Institutional populations such as mental hospitals and prisons, with their more challenging populations, have also had success with the use of reality therapy.

Reality therapy has specific goals. Its aim is to help patients find what they psychologically lack, such as feelings of belonging, freedom, power, and fun. The therapist meets with the patient to assess if his needs are being met, and works with him to attain these things, reestablishing or perhaps even establishing for the first time a positive life experience.

The importance of distraction in pain management is consistent with studies done in cognitive psychology, and there is more to come in the field of pain management as new ways of healing are increasingly chosen over more conventional forms of medicine.

NONTRADITIONAL MENTAL HEALTH THERAPY TECHNIQUES

Thus far this chapter has reviewed several of the more conventional forms of mental health therapy. Nontraditional medicine, however, also has a wide variety of therapies that are effective in treating many different kinds of mental illness and their symptoms.

Yoga

First practiced in India thousands of years ago, yoga experienced a resurgence in popularity in the 1990s. The different kinds of yoga are countless, and include Hatha yoga, Iyengar yoga, Sahaja yoga, and Kundalini yoga (one type of yoga made popular in the late 1990s by celebrities like Madonna).

Although often seen as a form of exercise, yoga is also used in many cultures as a way of maintaining physical as well as mental health. The benefits of yoga are found in the asanas, or poses, and in pranayama, or the breathing exercises. Both of these, if done properly and practiced regularly, can bring positive changes in the body. Although they may look easy, asanas are a challenge: in a subtle relationship between body and mind, they utilize several muscle groups at once and require a huge amount of concentration, focus, and strength.

Yoga is usually taught in small, intimate classes where close instructor-student interactions are encouraged. Under the instructor's guidance, the class is led through a series of asanas, usually ending in a pranayama or similar meditation-type form (sometimes called savasana) of relaxation.

There are obvious physical benefits to practicing yoga, such as an increase in muscle tone, strength, and flexibility, but this centuries-old practice also regulates and brings oxygen to all areas of the body. If there are problems in certain parts of the body, specific poses can be done to expedite the healing process in that area.

The breathing-exercise, meditative (pranayama) stage of the class may precede or follow the asanas. Sometimes a meditation or relaxation-like phase will occur both at the beginning and at the end of the class.

Yoga's main goal is to attain harmony and peace between the body, mind, and spirit; yoga means "union" in the ancient language of Sanskrit, and each pose is created to harmonize specific body systems and parts with the mind and spirit. One pose, for example, may have the benefits of strengthening the back muscles, but, if done properly, may also release repressed fear held in the body. Another pose urges along the cleaning process of the liver while it also lengthens the spine and carries fresh blood to the liver and brain.

How, then, does yoga work as a form of therapy? As yoga students practice yoga, incorporating both the asanas, and the meditation or breathing exercises, they will realize, over a few weeks, a decrease in anxiety levels, and a calming, "at peace" feeling. Studies have shown that people battling anxiety disorders, depression, and even psychosis have experienced an improvement in their mental health from practicing yoga. Of course, an improvement in one's physical appearance from the practice of yoga can boost one's self-confidence, but yoga can also bring a healthy feeling of order to the inside of the body as well.

PHARMACOTHERAPY

Pharmacotherapy, or drug therapy, is often used to treat those afflicted with mental illness. Whether to treat anxiety or depression or another more serious condition such as schizophrenia, there seems to be a pill for every affliction.

Drug therapy, when conducted under a doctor's supervision, can be a very effective way of combating many types of mental illness. Often, medication is used in conjunction with regular therapy sessions; to ensure that this safety step is taken, many insurance companies will not cover prescription costs unless the patient is under the care of a mental health professional. Also, drug therapy is often much more effective when combined with hard work done in a therapist's office: as a medication smoothes out and/or regulates the chemical imbalances in the brain, the patient is often better able to tackle difficult topics during therapy.

The field of drug therapy has progressed rapidly over a relatively short period of time. In the past, most antidepressants and antipsychotic drugs (often prescribed for conditions such as multiple personality disorder and psychosis), were slow to take effect and often left patients feeling zonked out and uncommunicative. The past decade or so has seen huge advancements in the distribution of new and improved drugs that are faster acting and more friendly on the patient.

After the initial excitement about drug therapy died down, however, people started to realize that antidepressants were being prescribed faster than pharmacists could keep them on the shelves. Doctors began to realize that a pill is not always the answer but that drug therapy can be very effective for some people when therapy alone does not work.

Generally the patient remains on the initial prescription until the therapist sees a marked improvement or decline in the patient's condition over a period of time, usually a few months. Then the therapist may suggest a change in medication (if a decline in mental health is experienced) or a decrease in dosage to test whether the patient's mental stability remains or fluctuates. A positive mood change can mean either the beginning of the end of the patient's drug therapy or the need for a change. Sometimes it takes a few tries with different medications until the right one is found. Sometimes the medication works for a while, but then becomes ineffective. Sometimes it's a matter of adjusting the patient's dosage or adding a supplementary medication to the therapy plan.

Drug therapy can produce positive results if done correctly. Whatever the case, patience, an open mind, and a comfortable doctor-patient relationship are keys to finding the right drug therapy.

The goals of yoga are a union of body, mind, and spirit. This can take years of discipline, and people looking for a way to lessen depression may not care about attaining that union. One can take from a yoga class whatever part one wants, whether it is a break from chronic anxiety attacks during pranayama or a lift in depression during an asana.

[For more information on yoga, see Chapter 10: Alternative Medicine.]

Meditation

Contrary to popular belief, meditation is much more than just sitting quietly. In fact, learning how to meditate is hard work. The benefits of what looks like just sitting still, however, can have lasting effects. This age-old practice has even found popularity among those looking for help with their mental illnesses.

Therapists report that people who meditate have felt decreases in their anxiety and stress levels, addictive behaviors, and depressions. Sometimes meditation is practiced in conjunction with other nontraditional therapy techniques, such as yoga. However it is practiced, the most important aspect of meditation is concentration.

Another form of nontraditional therapy is pet therapy, whereby an animal (usually a dog or cat) is used to help a person learn to relate to others or learn to love and feel love. (Photograph by Robert J. Huffman. Field Mark Publications. Reproduced by permission.)

To attain the intense concentration needed for effective meditation, patients will often choose an object, word, or phrase on which to focus, and center all attention on that thing. Some kinds of meditation incorporate props, such as lit candles, for focusing. Other kinds suggest repeating a word or phrase over and over, such as "ohm," which is used in Hindu traditions. Any word, though, will do; some people will repeat the word "love" or "peace." One should choose a word that supports an intense focus and full concentration; what is important is that one remains focused on the repetition. Once concentration is attained, the next step, or unbroken attention (meditation), should follow. (It is important to note here that getting to this point is a challenge. With meditation, patience is a virtue. Also, if the person finds his thoughts wandering from the chosen focus, which is normal, he should allow the uninterrupted thoughts to enter and then leave the mind, followed by a gentle self-guide back to the original word, phrase, or object.) Once this state of meditation is reached, a higher state of consciousness, sometimes called contemplation, is the next level. This may not be necessary for the beginner; benefits will still be felt if this higher consciousness is not immediately attained.

IT IS IMPORTANT TO NOTE THAT ALTHOUGH YOGA AND MEDITATION CAN BE VERY BENEFICIAL IN MAINTAINING AND IMPROVING MENTAL HEALTH, THEY ARE NOT SUBSTITUTES FOR MENTAL HEALTH THERAPY CONDUCTED UNDER MEDICAL SUPERVISION.

For those seeking help with their mental health, meditation can be a great way to increase focus and reduce anxiety and other mood disorders. Meditation is not something that can be practiced once with expected results; yoga and other nontraditional medical techniques require focus, patience, and dedication. The benefits, though, can greatly outweigh the hard work for someone who would like to add it to a mental health therapy plan.

[For more information on meditation, see Chapter 10: Alternative Medicine and Chapter 14: Habits and Behaviors.]

Bioenergetics (Body/Mind Therapy)

Bioenergetics, also called body/mind therapy, is a body-related psychotherapy developed by American doctor Alexander Lowen. Lowen was a student of Wilhelm Reich, who was a famous Austrian psychotherapist.

Influenced by Reich's theories, Lowen argued that the body, mind, and spirit are all interdependent and reflective. By practicing special exercises and verbal therapy, the body and mind can free itself from negative actions, called restrictive holding patterns. Bioenergetic therapists try to help their patients reach this freedom of body and mind.

Bioenergetics is based on a belief that personality is made of biological urges and conscious thought, or will. Lowen believed that emotional problems develop when a person fails to follow biological impulses except when there is a personal sense of desire. In other words, emotional problems can erupt when biological impulses are not consciously expressed because of fear. Lowen thought that neuroses were a form of defense, but with those neuroses comes a restraint of the true self. Through bioenergetic exercises meant to loosen rigid muscles, the defenses can be broken down and the true self can emerge. This also increases the amount of psychophysical energy (energy from the body and the mind); Lowen calls this bioenergy.

Breaking down this defense occurs gradually and, as the body feels more alive, repressed feelings are released and the neurosis is lessened. The verbal therapy aspect of the technique happens throughout the defense-lifting process, allowing the person to combine new thoughts and physical feelings into his life.

The bioenergetics technique begins with the therapist and patient engaging in some conversation, but then moving directly into the exercises, or bodywork. Patients work in close-fitting clothing so the therapist can see how the body changes as it moves. The exercises include lying, sitting, and standing in ways that increase the areas of stress in the body. Deep breathing during the session is encouraged because it pulls a large amount of bioenergy into the body, releasing repressed emotions. This energy is compared to an electric current, and can actually be seen by both therapist and patient as vibrations in muscles.

CHOOSING A THERAPIST

Deciding to begin therapy can be a big enough decision, but deciding whom to use as a therapist can be just as difficult. Talking to someone one hardly knows, about personal subjects, is difficult for anyone. Finding the right therapist can take time and patience until one feels the right connection.

Finding a therapist may require a bit of detective work. One's general practitioner is a good person to ask for the names of prospective therapists, as well as school guidance counselors, ministers, or rabbis. Some universities and colleges also have graduate therapy programs where, as part of their studies, graduate students offer quality psychotherapy for milder cases of emotional upset. This is a more affordable form of therapy, and these graduate programs will also often have lists of therapists in the area.

There are options, too, when deciding what kind of therapist to choose. A psychiatrist, along with being a therapist, is also a medical doctor, and can prescribe medication. Someone with "CSW" or "MSW" after his or her name has a master's degree in social work, and also works as a therapist, but cannot prescribe medication. Both kinds of therapists are board-certified and capable of providing quality care to the person in need. Sometimes a patient develops a need for medication while seeing a therapist; then an additional relationship may be introduced between the patient and a psychiatrist who can prescribe and monitor a drug therapy plan for the patient. The psychiatrist and therapist will work together, along with the patient, toward improving the patient's well-being.

The important thing to remember when choosing a therapist is that it is okay to be selective; this relationship requires trust, mutual respect, sensitivity, and understanding. Only then can a patient's goals be reached.

Throughout the exercises, the bioenergetic therapist might touch or massage certain areas of the patient's body that seem to resist release. At certain points during the session, the patient is also reminded to make sounds (as part of the verbal therapy); the release of sounds sends more bioenergy through the body.

Since the release of defenses in the body happens over a period of time and not all at once, bioenergetics is a long-term therapy, but for many it is the answer to controlling or combating feelings of anxiety, depression, or other kinds of emotional upset.

Creative Arts Therapies

A creative arts therapy is a technique that utilizes some form of creative expression as a way of producing a change in one's mental health. Some of these therapies include art, drama, dance, poetry, and music. Through these mediums one can express oneself in nonverbal ways. The results of this form of therapy are an increase in self-esteem, self-expression, and improved social interactions.

The quality of the patient's expression, whether it is a painting or a dance routine, does not matter in these creative therapies; what matters is the significance learned from the work for both therapist and patient and how this new knowledge can help the patient. To this end, creative arts therapists do not participate too much in sessions so as not to interrupt the patient's self-expression and self-realization.

Creative therapies are usually conducted in hospitals and institutions for the mentally challenged. Some creative arts therapists work together with other psychotherapists; in fact, these therapies were influenced to an extent by psychoanalysis and take a psychoanalytic angle in their techniques. In addition, all of them can be used in conjunction with other, more conventional therapy techniques.

ART THERAPY. Art therapy is used to help patients overcome emotional conflicts and become more self-aware. To do this, the art therapist will guide patients in the use of certain art materials, such as pastels or crayons, to express themselves, but clay, paper, or finger paints may also be used, depending on the issue being addressed. These specially selected materials can be used to express what is in patients' minds before they are able to put it into words. (Sometimes art is an easier form of expression for patients than verbalizing their pain.)

Art therapy can provide a positive feeling of expression within patients as well as allow a physical release of creative energy as work is being created. If a specific topic is not immediately apparent, the therapist might suggest a topic for expression, such as one's family or a vivid childhood memory.

This drawing was done by an autistic boy, who expresses his friendship with another boy by drawing the two together in a car. (*American Journal of Art Therapy*, Volume 27, No. 2. Reproduced by permission of Gladys Agell and Vermont College of Norwich University.)

Over the past decade, art therapists have added other mediums to their techniques, such as music or movement. These additions have been helpful with the recent inclusion of creative art therapy work with incest survivors, prisoners, and victims of war. An ever-expanding therapy form, art therapy can be a constructive alternative to conventional mental health therapies.

[For more information on art therapists, see Chapter 6: Health Care Careers.]

DANCE THERAPY. Using the freedom of movement, dance therapy can help patients interrelate psychological and physiological processes. Actual dance techniques are not usually taught, though; instead, patients are urged to express themselves through virtually any form of movement, no matter how spontaneous. Therapists' approaches to patients have to be creative, but must also result from observation of patients' immediate needs through signs like physical tension. The dance or art therapist may also copy patients' actions to relay understanding over certain situations. Following that, patients may be asked to respond verbally or to keep moving. The use of rhythm and energy can also be helpful for patients who need to remove both physical and emotional tension.

Art therapy can help people cope with post-traumatic stress disorder. Pictured is a child's drawing of the 1986 *Challenger* space shuttle, which exploded seconds after take-off. (*Exceptional Children, Exceptional Art: Teaching Art to Special Needs.* Reproduced by permission of David R. Henley.)

Dance therapy has shown success with everyone from professional dancers to autistic children. It allows patients to feel emotional and physiological feelings at the same time and to convey them in a secure, constructive setting.

MUSIC THERAPY. Music has been part of human culture more or less since the beginning of time. It has played an integral part in the history of mankind. It has also been associated in the past as having power; in ancient Greece, for example, it was thought to have a special force over one's physical and emotional self. In addition, music has also played a significant role in cultural and religious services. It makes sense, then, that music could be used in therapy.

Today, the calming effect from music is still a by-product of music therapy. Music therapists use the power of music to identify and deal with a wide range of emotional disturbances—everything from drug abuse to schizophrenia and Alzheimer's disease.

There is a wide variety of music therapy approaches; the one to choose is a personal preference. Most music therapists have musical instruments available for patients to use during sessions in their quest for self-expression. Using these instruments, exercises are conducted, led by the therapist, which aid in the process of uncovering conflict. Often, patients are encouraged to act out spontaneous expressions, even if they might interfere with an exercise. The instruments can also be used as props to describe and act out certain situations. In a classic example, a patient might be asked to choose and then manipulate instruments that remind him or her of family members or difficult situations or feelings.

As this therapy technique grows, music therapists continue to learn more about music and its therapeutic benefits. New age music, for example, has been found to help those engaged in self-destructive behavior. Undoubtedly, more is to come from this creative art therapy.

PSYCHODRAMA. Psychodrama, another creative arts therapy technique, has shown to be a very effective therapy when used with other forms of psychotherapy and in crisis intervention.

In psychodrama, the therapist and patient approach a problem as if they were director and playwright, which allows the patient more interactions with the issue and the conquering of the conflict. By acting out their problems, patients also experience a deeper level of awareness.

Developed in the 1930s by Viennese psychiatrist J. L. Moreno (1889–1974), psychodrama has been found to show positive effects on posttraumatic stress disorder, substance abuse, and other conditions requiring long-term hospitalization. The range of materials used can be anything from classic forms of playwriting, such as Shakespeare, to simpler forms of theater, such as puppet shows. In psychodrama sessions, the therapist keeps close tabs on patients and establishes just the right relationship with them. A patient, for example, might act out a submissive character, such as a mouse, whereas the therapist chooses to be a dominant animal, such as a cat, and acts out that character while observing the patient's reactions. The drama therapist works hard in sessions and goes beyond classic role-playing techniques to work as actor and director.

The goal of psychodrama is for the patient, through acting, to enact life conflicts and derive self-awareness and growth from this acting. Other benefits of psychodrama include an increase in creativity and interpersonal skills and an increased awareness in one's feelings and emotions.

Hypnotherapy

Hypnosis is an altered state of awareness, much like daydreaming or being so involved in a task that one loses track of time; these are altered states into which all our minds occasionally fall. Hypnosis can be beneficial in therapy, and, in a therapeutic setting, is often accompanied by physical relaxation, which can be very helpful when uncovering topics that produce stress.

There are two approaches to hypnotherapy: the permissive and the indirect. The hypnotherapist using the permissive technique treats patients as equals, gently instructing them that they may move along with the hypnosis process if desired (for example, "You may take a deep breath now, if you wish"). The hypnotherapist using the indirect approach, however, would say, "Take a deep breath now." The indirect technique is different from the permissive one in another way: it does not use a formal hypnosis procedure (see below) and the patient is usually unaware that the procedure is happening.

After the initial interview between therapist and patient and an explanation of the realities of hypnosis (for example, that the therapist does not have complete control over the patient's brain, as the media often portrays), the therapist will induce the hypnotic state. This is done through visual imagery; the patient pictures a relaxing situation and is instructed to relive that situation and feeling as much as possible. When the patient reaches some level of trance (often reached while listening to the therapist verbalize the visualization techniques), depending on the level of hypnosis, the patient can recall certain repressed memories. Some patients need deep levels of hypnosis to recall past experiences; others can benefit from light hypnosis.

Although not a form of psychotherapy itself, hypnotherapy can be used with other forms of psychotherapy to combat anxiety disorders, multiple personality disorder, psychosis, and other mental disturbances.

THERAPY FORMATS

After deciding that therapy fits one's needs, the next step is deciding what form of therapy is best. There are a few types, and their characteristics are featured below.

Individual Therapy

Often the first form of counseling encountered by first-time therapy seekers, individual therapy is made up of sessions between a therapist and patient. The sessions are usually held on a regular basis, and, depending on the kind of therapy chosen, sessions can occur anywhere from one to four times a week. Details of individual therapy sessions (that is, the positions of the patient and therapist in the room, the duration of a session, the nature of the therapist-patient relationship, etc.) vary across different therapy types.

Many patients prefer individual therapy to other forms of therapy because of the one-on-one attention received from the therapist. For others, it may be hard enough for them to express themselves with their therapist, but add a few more people in the room and the patient may feel very uncomfortable and not at all like talking.

Individual therapy is often suggested for first-time patients to fully introduce the therapy experience in a gentle, personal manner. The patient may then move on to other forms (discussed below) or even add a second therapy form to his or her initial therapy plan.

Couples Therapy/Family Therapy

Couples or marital (marriage) therapy is often paired with family therapy because of the similar topics discussed in both forms. Today, the term "couples" is used more often than "marital," however, to include the growing number of people who live together in a committed relationship but are not yet married or choose not to marry. Couples therapy and family therapy will be discussed together here because of their similarities.

In both couples and family therapy, the relationship between therapist and patient is not as important as the relationship and interaction between the couple or family members. The goal is to allow the patient to see the partner or family member as he or she really is and not as a product of the patient's repressed emotions about that person. Usually, a conflict between a couple or between family members is a sign of an emotional difficulty in one member of the couple or family; the therapist works to figure out what that conflict might be. Sex therapy, too, is often part of couples therapy, as sexual problems between partners are a common problem; when other conflicts arise within the relationship, a couple's sex life will likely be affected.

In couples and family sessions, patients are encouraged to listen to each other with empathy and to be clear in relaying what they think is being said by the other patient(s) and what feelings surround this. The therapist's awareness of which stage each patient is in in the relationship (at the beginning of a conflict versus being at a point where a partner or family member is considering leaving the relationship), is also important in planning the therapy strategy. Despite who in the relationship is suffering the most, it is the therapist's duty to be sensitive to the needs of all patients involved.

Group Therapy

Group therapy was first introduced in 1905 by American internist Joseph A. Pratt, who developed this therapy technique for patients suffering from tuberculosis (an infectious lung disease) so they could share concerns and support one another. The concept gained popularity through the 1930s, and in 1948 the American Group Psychotherapy Association was formed.

Before entering group therapy, the interested patient meets with the group therapist so the therapist can get to know the patient and learn his background, and the patient can get a feel for what the group sessions will be like. Groups usually meet once a week for one to two hours. (Groups meeting within a larger institution gather for shorter periods, however, because persons in these facilities are often severely disturbed and cannot focus for long periods of time.)

Once in the group meeting, the hour begins either with one person opening the conversation or with an opening from the therapist. Much less involved than in other therapy forms, the group therapist acts more as mediator, referee, and time clock than anything else. What is important is to get group members to interact among themselves in a constructive manner. Sometimes all members of the group participate, sometimes not, depending on the topic or group members' attitudes that session.

The dynamics of group therapy sessions are in themselves part of the healing process for a patient. Often patients can learn about themselves

Teenage males attending a group therapy session. (Photograph © 1992 Kevin Beebe. Custom Medical Stock Photo. Reproduced by permission.)

through other patients' experiences. Also, social pressures are at their strongest in these sessions. For example, the therapist's suggesting that patient A is acting aggressive is more believable to that patient if patients B, C, and D agree with the therapist. It is also comforting for many patients to be engaged with those who are sharing their problems and life upheavals.

For many people, group therapy is just as effective as individual therapy. Researchers have found that since one's personality is based primarily on interactions with others, therapists can learn about the patients in a group therapy session by observing their interactions with other patients. Treatment, then, for one patient in the group can be based on the therapist's observations of that patient during the group session.

Support Groups

Created out of a need to educate and protect, a support group exists as a way to help people afflicted with the same or similar problems and conditions in a group setting. Countless support groups have surfaced in recent years. Some are not as serious as others, but many have enlightened and provided support for hundreds of thousands of people.

ALCOHOLICS ANONYMOUS (AA). Based partly on the studies of cognitive therapists and techniques of rational-emotive behavior therapy (REBT), Alcoholics Anonymous (AA) has provided help to millions of people who suffer from alcoholism. AA is based on a twelve-step program for restructuring one's life as an addict; in these twelve steps addicts admit to, come to terms with, and hopefully conquer their addictions. AA also acts as a comforting support network for alcoholics and recovering alcoholics in the effort to become, and stay, clean and sober.

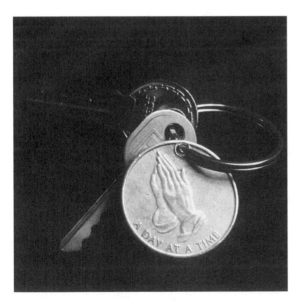

Key ring with the inscription "A Day at A Time," given to recovering alcoholics at Alcoholics Anonymous as a symbol of their continuing recovery. (Photograph by Robert J. Huffman. Field Mark Publications. Reproduced by permission.)

AA and the twelve-step program paved the way for numerous substance-abuse or other kinds of support groups, such as Narcotics Anonymous, Gamblers Anonymous, Overeaters Anonymous, and Bulimics Anonymous. Offshoot support groups, such as Al-Anon, for alcoholics' loved ones, have also developed for the families, partners, and friends of addicts. (See Chapter 14: Habits and Behaviors, for more information on AA.)

Both the support and offshoot support groups can be very helpful for those battling addictive behaviors, whether it is the addicts or their families and friends. As with so many other therapy forms and techniques, joining a support group requires dedication, time and patience.

SELF-HELP

Battling and living with a mental illness or other emotional upset can be overwhelming and sometimes very painful. Even with therapy and other helpful techniques in the field of mental health, individuals can still feel alone and out of control of their emotions. This can be alleviated, however, by taking control of the situation and adopting additional practices in life that can help to soften the edges of the daily struggle:

- Exercise: Exercise can greatly improve one's symptoms when dealing with emotional disturbance. Not only does it promote good overall health and increase self-esteem and the quality of one's appearance, but it has also been shown to decrease levels of anxiety and depression in people who adopt a regular exercise plan.
- Sleep: Adequate sleep is crucial when living with a mental illness. During sleep one's body systems have a chance to rebuild, replenish, and rest themselves, which is vital in maintaining a healthy body and mind.
- Eat properly: This can be tough; today's busy schedules make it difficult to get five fruits and vegetables into a diet each day. But just as sleep is essential to maintaining the body, a healthful diet can provide the brainpower and physical energy needed to live life fully.
- Follow a mental health plan: Whether one lives with an anxiety disorder or full-blown clinical depression, it is important to follow the mental health plan arranged between patient and therapist.

FOR MORE INFORMATION

Books

Gorman, Jack M. *The Essential Guide to Mental Health: The Most Comprehensive Guide to the Psychiatry for Popular Family Use.* Griffith Trade Paperback, 1998.

Bibliography

BOOKS

General

Adderholt-Elliot, Miriam and Jan Goldberg. *Perfectionism: What's Bad About Being Too Good.* Minneapolis, MN: Free Spirit Publishing, 1999.

Davitz, Lois Jean, Joel R. Davitz, Lois Leiderman Davitz, and Jo Davitz. *20 Tough Questions Teenagers Ask: And 20 Tough Answers.* Minneapolis, MN: Paulist Press, 1998.

Holm, Sharon Lane (Illustrator) and Faith Hickman Brynie. *101 Questions Your Brain Has Asked About Itself but Couldn't Answer. . .Until Now.* Brookfield, CT: Millbrook Press, 1998.

Kalergis, Mary Motley. *Seen and Heard: Teenagers Talk About Their Lives.* New York: Stewart Tabori & Chang, 1998.

McCoy, Ph.D., Kathy, and Charles Wibbelsman, M.D.(Contributor). *Life Happens: A Teenager's Guide to Friends, Failure, Sexuality, Love, Rejection, Addiction, Peer Pressure, Families, Loss, Depression, Change and Other Challenges of Living.* Perigee Paperbacks, 1996.

Parsley, Bonnie M., Scott Peck. *The Choice Is Yours: A Teenager's Guide to Self Discovery, Relationships, Values, and Spiritual Growth.* New York: Fireside, 1992.

Roehm, Michelle (Editor) and Marci Doane Roth (Illustrator). *Girls Know Best: Advice for Girls from Girls on Just About Everything.* Beyond Words Pub. Co., 1997.

Roehm, Michelle (Editor) and Marianne Monson-Burton (Editor). *Boys Know It All: Wise Thoughts and Wacky Ideas From Guys Just Like You.* Beyond Words Pub. Co., 1998.

Turner, Priscilla (Editor), and Susan Pohlmann (Editor). *A Boy's Guide to Life: The Complete Instructions.* New York: Penguin USA, 1997.

Eating Disorders

Chiu, Christina. *Eating Disorder Survivors Tell Their Stories.* (The Teen Health Library of Eating Disorder Prevention). Minneapolis, MN: Hazelden Information Education, 1999.

Davis, Brangien. *What's Real, What's Ideal: Overcoming a Negative Body Image.* (The Teen Health Library of Eating Disorder Prevention). Minneapolis, MN: Hazelden Information Education, 1999.

Erlanger, Ellen. *Eating Disorders: A Question and Answer Book About Anorexia Nervosa and Bulima Nervosa.* Minneapolis, MN: Lerner Publications Company, 1988.

Frissell, Susan and Paula Harney. *Eating Disorders and Weight Control.* (Issues in Focus). Springfield, NJ: Enslow Publishers, Inc., 1998.

Harmon, Dan and Carol C. Nadelson. *Anorexia Nervosa: Starving for Attention.* (Encyclopedia of Psychological Disorders). New York: Chelsea House Publishers, 1998.

Kaminker, Laura. *Exercise Addiction: When Fitness Becomes an Obsession.* (The Teen Health Library of Eating Disorder Prevention). Minneapolis, MN: Hazelden Information Education, 1999.

Kolodny, Nancy J. *When Food's a Foe: How You Can Confront and Conquer Your Eating Disorder.* Boston, MA: Little Brown & Co., 1998.

Moe, Barbara. *Understanding the Causes of a Negative Body Image.* Hazelden Information Education. Minneapolis, MN: Hazelden Information Education, 1999.

Monroe, Judy. *Understanding Weight-Loss Programs: A Teen Eating Disorder Prevention Book.* Minneapolis, MN: Hazelden Information Education, 1999.

Patterson, Charles. *Eating Disorders (Teen Hot Line).* Chatham, NJ: Raintree/Steck Vaughn, 1995.

Smith, Erica. *Anorexia Nervosa: When Food is the Enemy.* Minneapolis, MN: Hazelden Information Education, 1999.

Sneddon, Pamela Shires. *Body Image: A Reality Check.* (Issues in Focus.) Springfield, NJ: Enslow Publishers, Inc., 1999.

Stanley, Debbie. *Understanding Anorexia Nervosa.* Minneapolis, MN: Hazelden Information Education, 1999.

Stanley, Debbie. *Understanding Bulimia Nervosa.* Minneapolis, MN: Hazelden Information Education, 1999.

Habits and Behaviors

Connelly, Elizabeth Russell, Beth Connolly, and Carol C. Nadelson. *Through a Glass Darkly: The Psychological Effects of Marijuana and Hashish.* (Encylopedia of Psychological Disorders). New York: Chelsea House Publishers, 1999.

Holmes, Ann, Carol C. Nadelson (Editor), and Claire E. Reinburg (Editor). *Cutting the Pain Away: Understanding Self-Mutilation.* (Encyclopedia of Psychological Disorders). New York: Chelsea House Publishers, 1999.

Klein, Wendy. *Drugs and Denial.* (Drug Abuse Prevention Library). New York: The Rosen Publishing Group, 1998.

Peacock, Nancy, Carol C. Nadelson (Editor), and Claire E. Reinburg. *Drowning Our Sorrows: Psychological Effects of Alcohol Abuse.* New York: Chelsea House Publishers, 1999.

Snyder, Solomon H. (Editor) and P. Mick Richardson. *Flowering Plants: Magic in Bloom.* (Encyclopedia of Psychoactive Drugs, Series 1.) New York: Chelsea House Publishers, 1992.

Wilkinson, Beth. *Drugs and Depression.* Minneapolis, MN: Hazelden Information Education, 1997.

Mental Health

Adler, Joe Ann. *Stress: Just Chill Out!* (Teen Issues). Springfield, NJ: Enslow Publishers, 1997.

Barrett, Susan L., Pamela Espeland (Editor), and J. Urbanovic (Translator). *It's All in Your Head: A Guide to Understanding Your Brain and Boosting Your Brain Power.* Minneapolis, MN: Free Spirit Publishing, 1992.

Carlson, Dale Bick, Carol Nicklaus (Illustrator), and R. E. Mark Lee. *Stop the Pain: Teen Meditations.* Madison, CT: Bick Pub House, 1999.

Carlson, Dale Bick, Hannah Carlson, and Carol Nicklaus (Illustrator). *Where's Your Head?: Psychology for Teenagers.* Madison, CT: Bick Publishing House, 1998.

Espeland, Pamela and Elizabeth Verdick. *Making Every Day Count: Daily Readings for Young People on Solving Problems, Setting Goals, and Feeling Good About Yourself.* Minneapolis, MN: Free Spirit Publishing, 1998.

Hipp, Earl, Pamela Espeland, and Michael Fleishman (Illustrator). *Fighting Invisible Tigers: A Stress Management Guide for Teens.* Minneapolis, MN: Free Spirit Publishing, 1995.

Kincher, Jonni and Pamela Espeland (Editor). *Psychology for Kids II: 40 Fun Experiments That Help You Learn About Others.* Minneapolis, MN: Free Spirit Publishing, 1998.

Kincher, Jonni, Bach, Julie S. (Editor), and Steve Michaels (Illustrator). *Psychology for Kids: 40 Fun Tests That Help You Learn About Yourself.* Minneapolis, MN: Free Spirit Publishing, 1995.

Krulik, Nancy E. *Don't Stress! How To Keep Life's Problems Little.* New York: Scholastic Trade, 1998.

Miller, Shannon (Introduction), Nancy Ann Richardson (Contributor). *Winning Every Day: Gold Medal Advice for a Happy, Healthy Life!* New York: Bantam Doubleday Dell, 1998.

Packard, Gwen K. *Coping With Stress.* Minneapolis, MN: Hazelden Information Education, 1997.

Policoff, Stephen Phillip. *The Dreamer's Companion: A Young Person's Guide to Understanding Dreams and Using Them Creatively.* Chicago: Chicago Review Press, 1997.

Romain, Trevor and Elizabeth Verdick. *What on Earth Do You Do When Someone Dies?* Minneapolis, MN: Free Spirit Publishing, 1999.

Mental Illness

Connelly, Elizabeth Russell and Carol C. Nadelson. *Conduct Unbecoming: Hyperactivity, Attention Deficit, and Disruptive Behavior Disorders.* (Encyclopedia of Psychological Disorders). New York: Chelsea House Publishers, 1998.

Garland, E. Jane. *Depression Is the Pits, But I'm Getting Better: A Guide for Adolescents.* Washington, D.C.: Magination Press, 1998.

Gellman, Marc, Thomas Hartman, and Deborah Tilley (Illustrator). *Lost and Found: A Kid's Book for Living Through Loss.* New York: Morrow Junior, 1999.

Holmes, Ann, Dan Harmon, and Carol C. Nadelson (Editor). *The Tortured Mind: The Many Faces of Manic Depression.* (Encylopedia of Psychological Disorders). New York: Chelsea House Publishers, 1998.

Kaminker, Laura. *Exercise Addiction: When Fitness Becomes an Obsession.* (The Teen Health Library of Eating Disorder Prevention). Minneapolis, MN: Hazelden Information Education, 1999.

Moe, Barbara. *Understanding the Causes of a Negative Body Image.* Minneapolis, MN: Hazelden Information Education, 1999.

Monroe, Judy. *Phobias: Everything You Wanted to Know, but Were Afraid to Ask.* (Issues in Focus). Springfield, NJ: Enslow Publishers, Inc., 1996.

Nardo, Don. *Anxiety and Phobias.* (Encyclopedia of Psychological Disorders). New York: Chelsea House Publishers, 1992.

Porterfield, Kay Marie. *Straight Talk About Post-Traumatic Stress Disorder: Coping With the Aftermath of Trauma.* Checkmark Books, 1996.

Silverstein, Alvin, Virginia Silverstein, and Laura Silverstein Nunn. *Depression.* (Diseases and People.) Springfield, NJ: Enslow Publishers, Inc., 1997.

Wilkinson, Beth. *Drugs and Depression.* Minneapolis, MN: Hazelden Information Education, 1997.

Sexuality

Baer, Judy. *Dear Judy, Did You Ever Like a Boy (Who Didn't Like You?).* Minneapolis, MN: Bethany House, 1993.

Basso, Michael J. *The Underground Guide to Teenage Sexuality: An Essential Handbook for Today's Teens & Parents.* Minneapolis, MN: Fairview Press, 1997.

Carlson, Dale Bick, Hannah Carlson, and Carol Nicklaus (Illustrator). *Girls Are Equal Too: How to Survive Guide for Teenage Girls.* Madison, CT: Bick Pub House, 1998.

Fenwick, Elizabeth and Robert Walker. *How Sex Works: A Clear, Comprehensive Guide for Teenagers to Emotional, Physical, and Sexual Maturity.* DK Publishing, 1994.

Gravelle, Karen, Nick Castro (Contributor), Chava Castro, and Robert Leighton (Illustrator). *What's Going on Down There: Answers to Questions Boys Find Hard to Ask.* New York: Walker & Co., 1998.

Harris, Robie H. *It's Perfectly Normal: Changing Bodies, Growing Up, Sex, and Sexual Health.* Candlewick Press, 1994.

Pogany, Susan Browning. *Sex Smart: 501 Reasons to Hold Off on Sex.* Minneapolis, MN: Fairview Press, 1998.

WEB SITES

ADOL: Adolescence Directory On-Line. http://education.indiana.edu/cas/adol/adol.html

The American Dietetic Association. http://www.eatright.org

Better Health. http://www.betterhealth.com

Centers for Disease Control and Prevention. http://www.cdc.com

Channel One. http://channelone.com/

The Children's Health Center. http://www.mediconsult.com/mc/mcsite.nsf/conditionnav/kids~sectionintroduction

Club Drugs (National Institute on Drug Abuse). http://www.clubdrugs.org

CyberDiet. http://www/cyberdiet.com

Drug-Free Resource Net (Partnership for a Drug-Free America). http://drugfreeamerica.org

bibliography

Healthfinder. http://www.healthfinder.gov

InteliHealth: Home to Johns Hopkins Health Information. http://www.intelihealth.com

Mayo Clinic Health Oasis. http://mayohealth.org

On Health. http://www.onhealth.com

Prevention Online (National Clearinghouse for Alcohol and Drug Information). http://www.health.org

The Vegetarian Resource Group. http://www.vrg.org

Index

Italic type indicates volume number; **boldface** type indicates main entries and their page numbers; (ill.) indicates photos and illustrations.